I am grateful to God for everything! And I believe that the meaning of life is to give meaning to other lives. R.E.A, you are the meaning of my life.
Love you

Danielly Vieira
2024

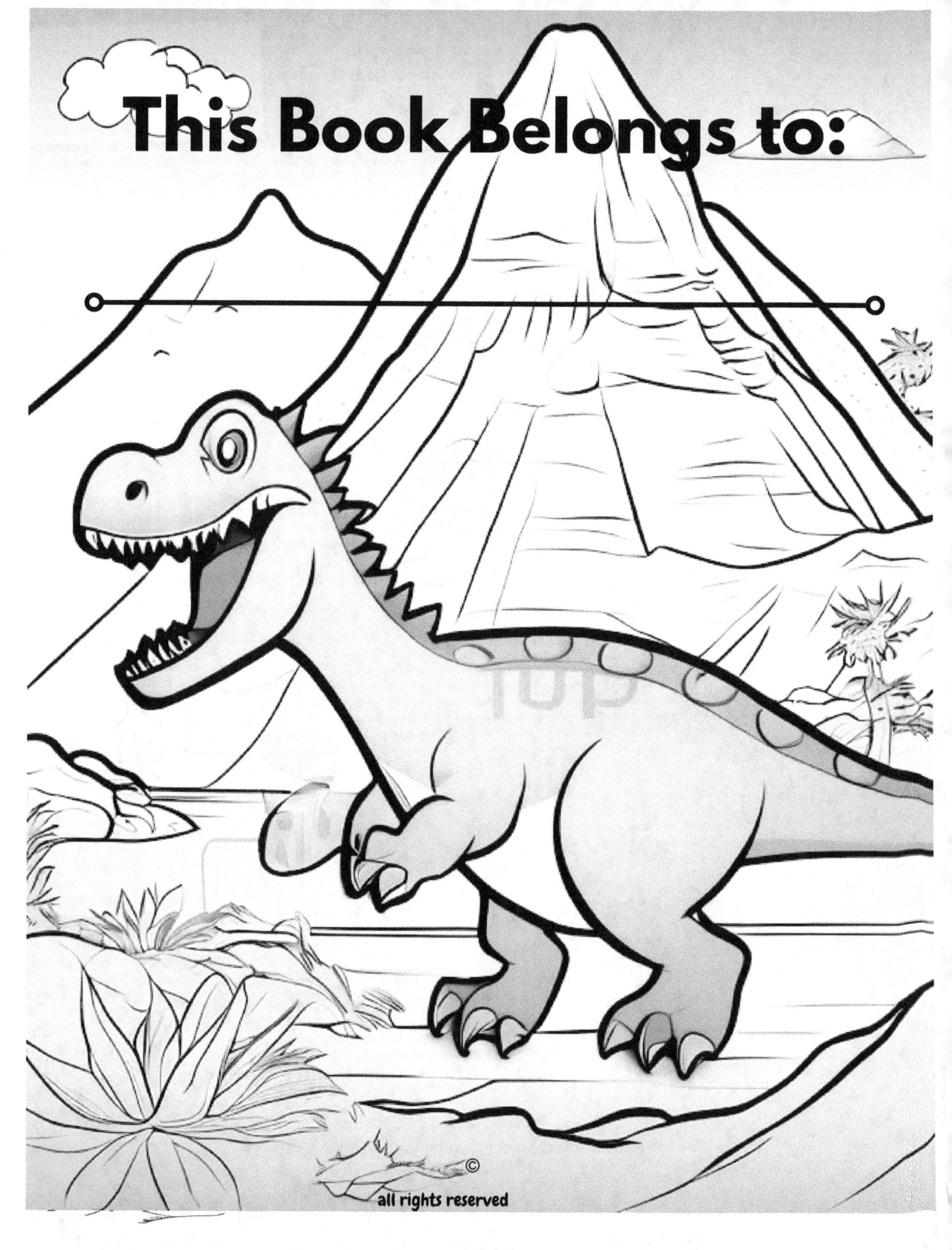

This Book Belongs to:

Test Color Page

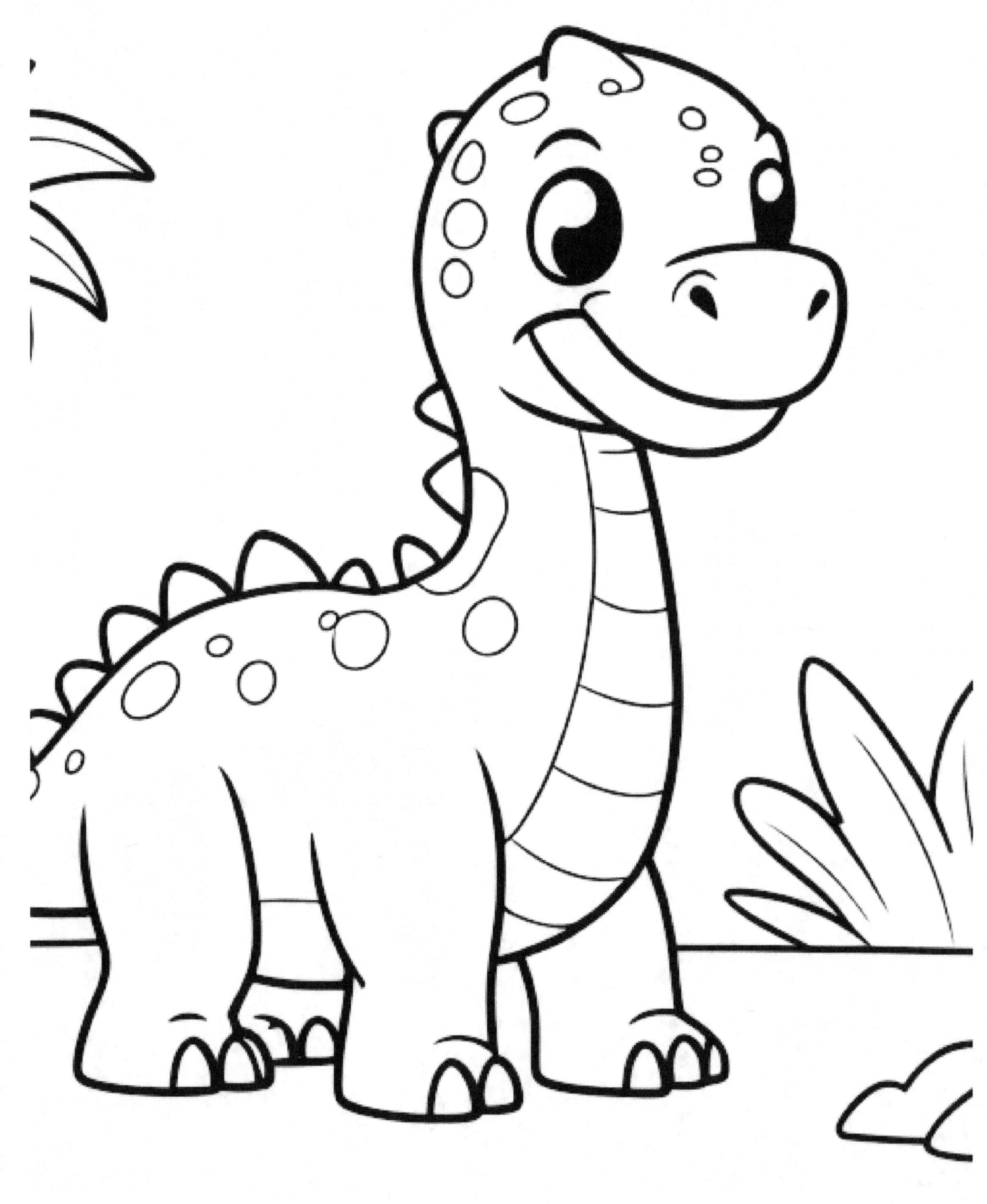

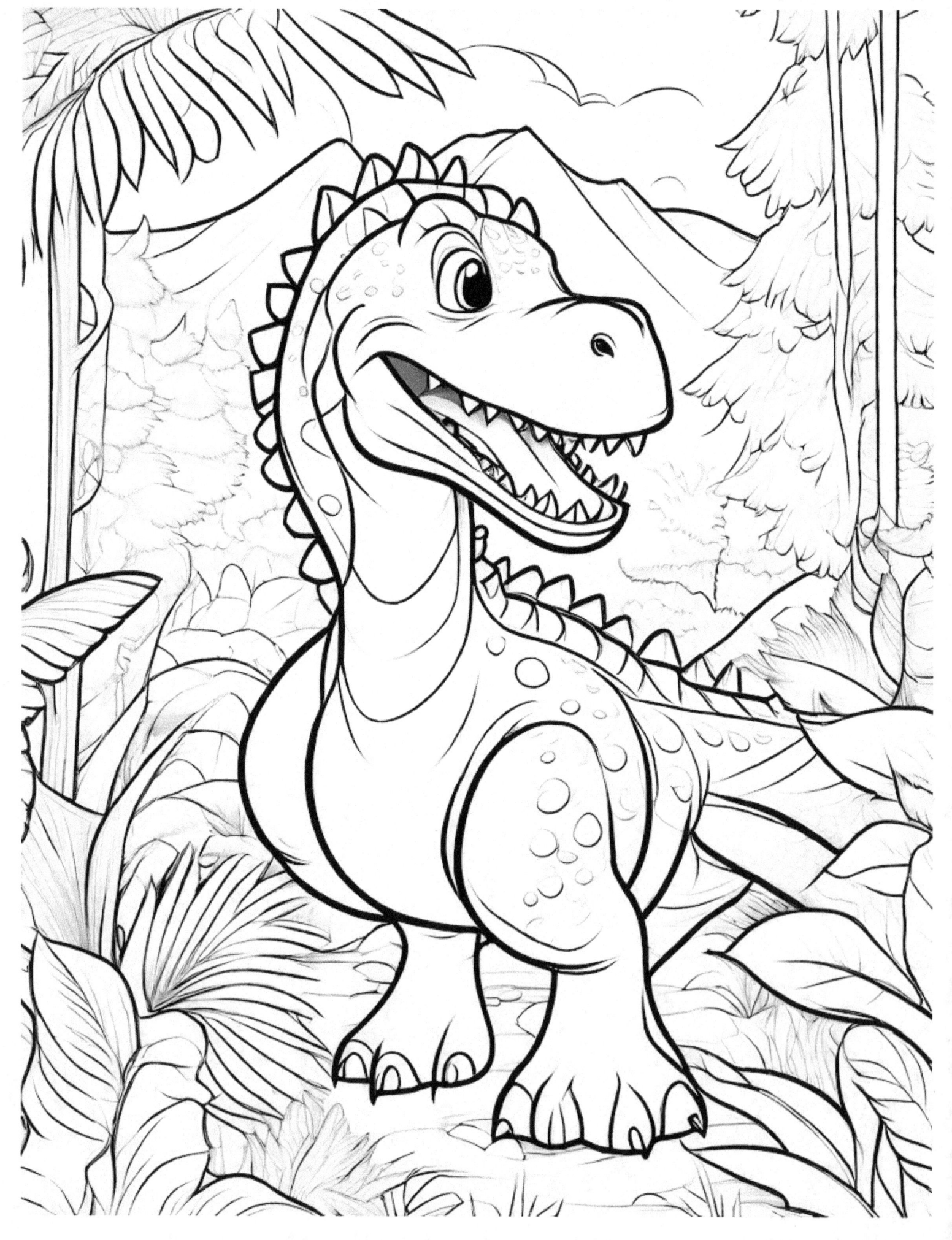

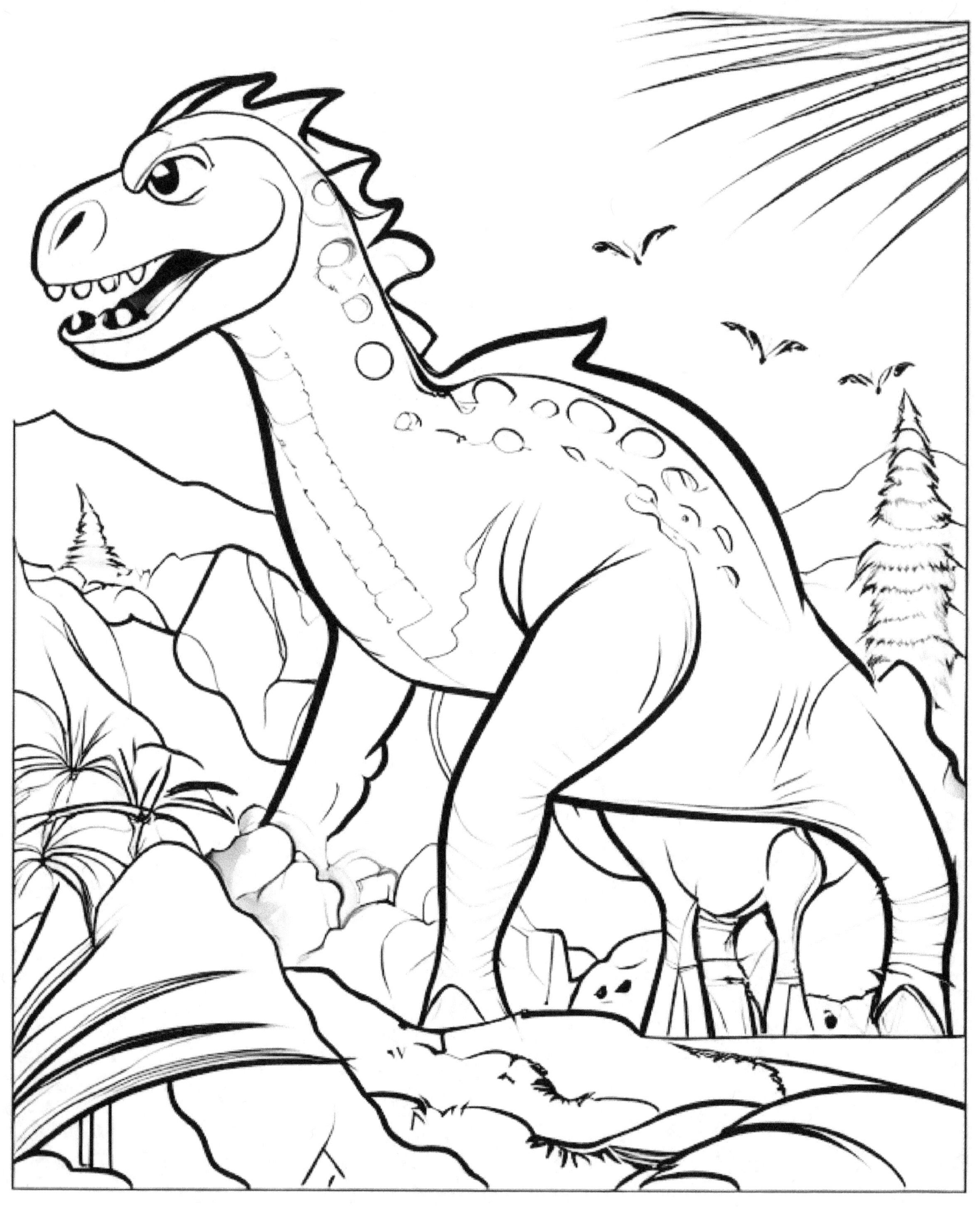

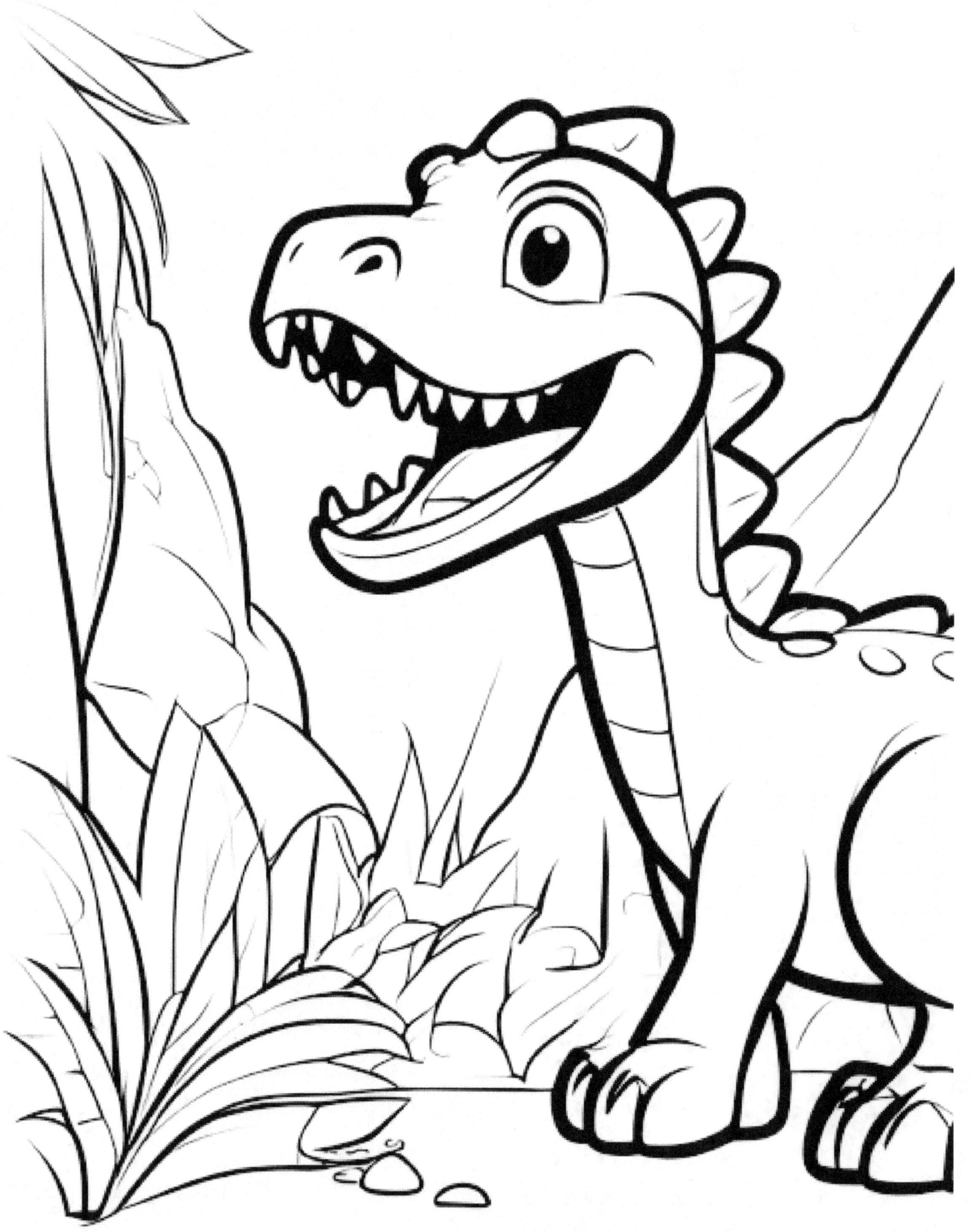

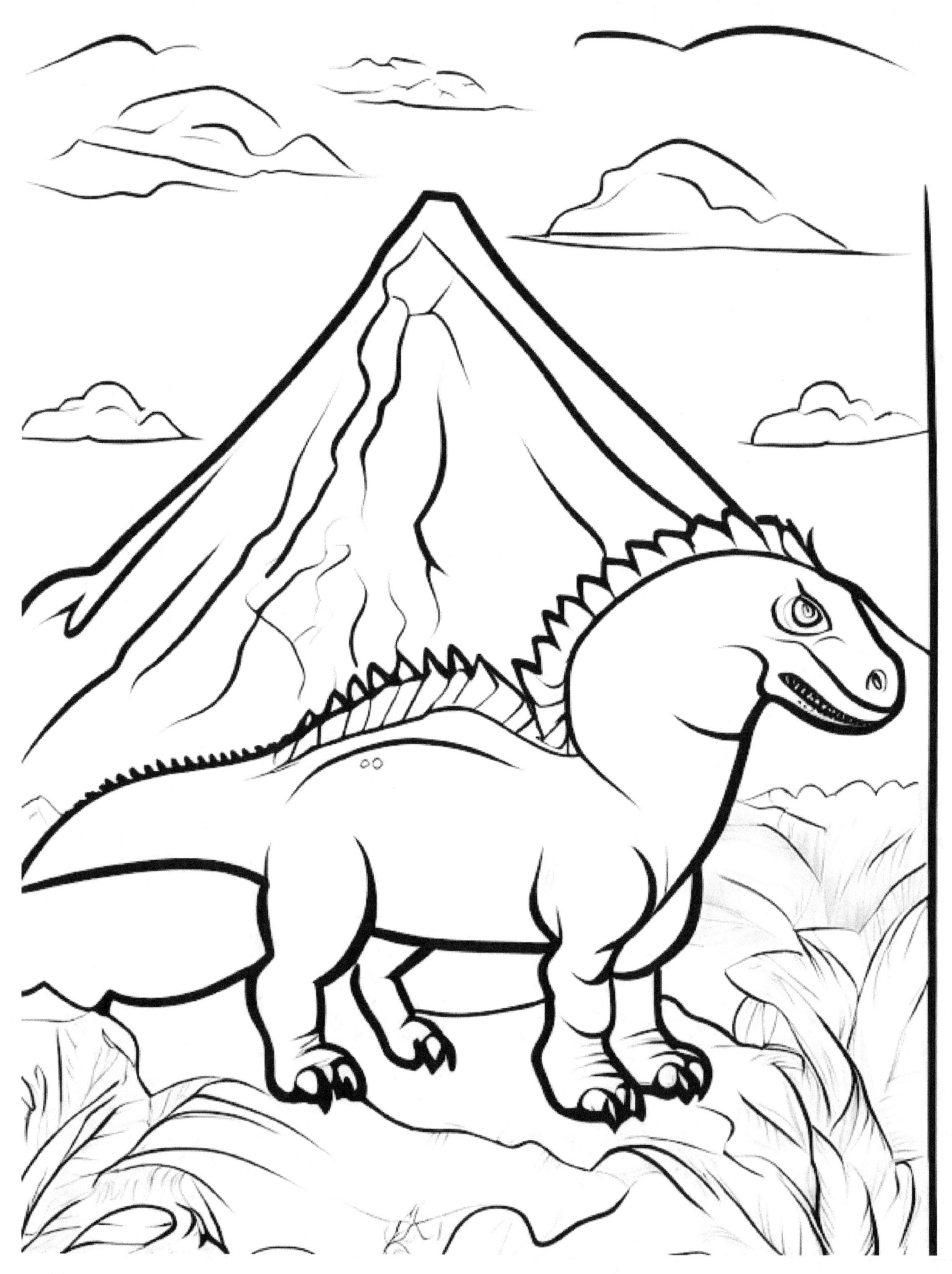

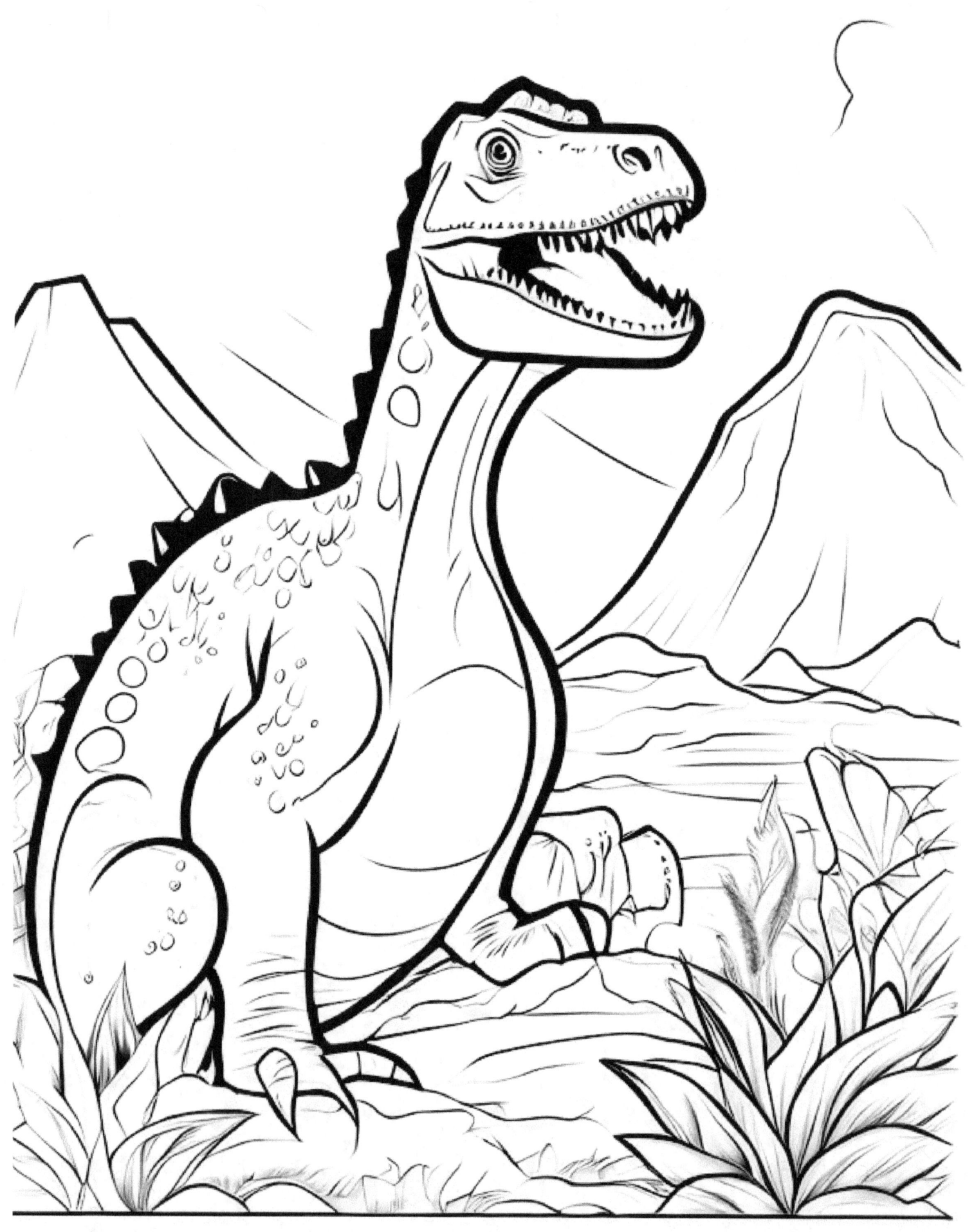

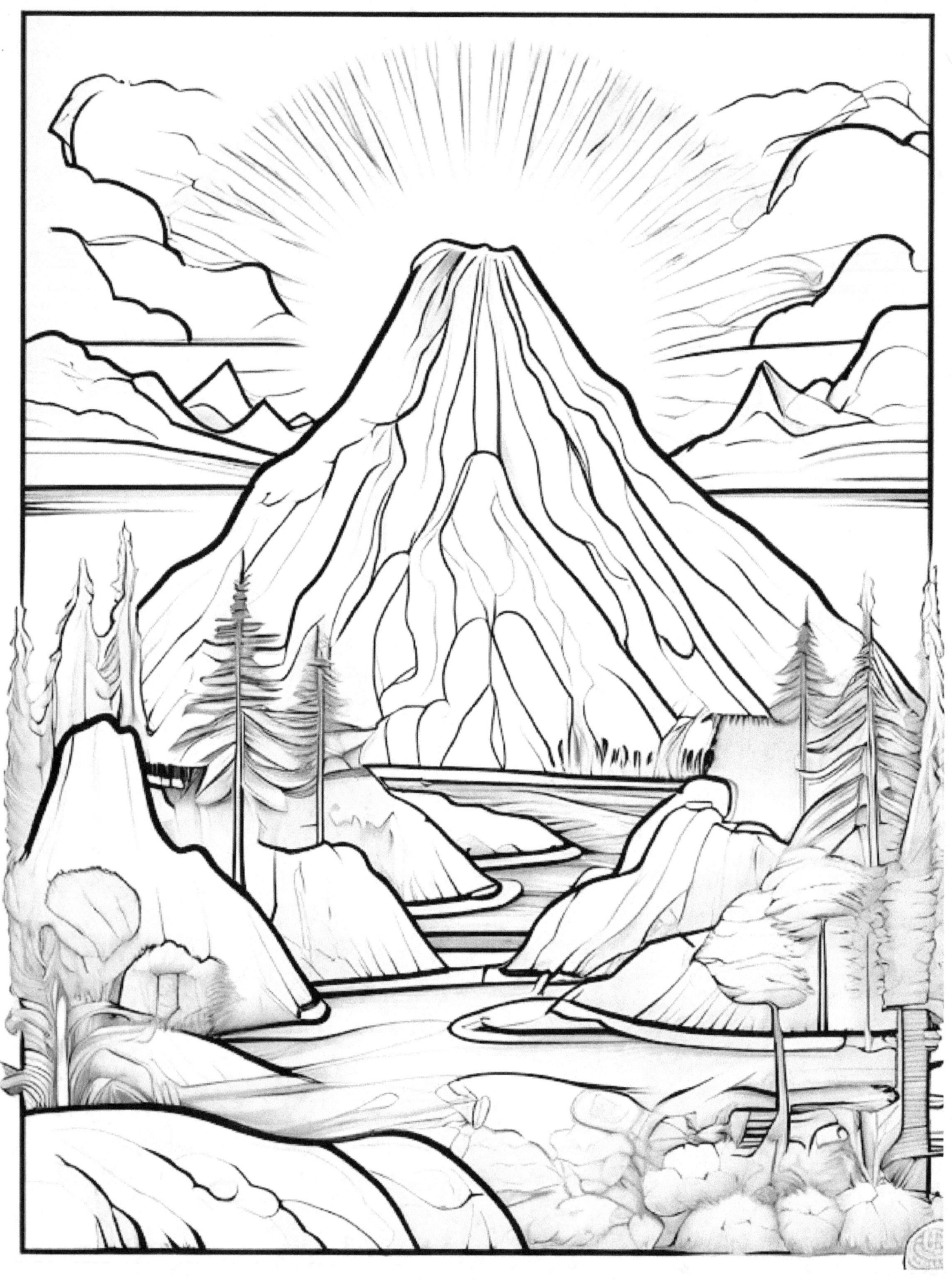

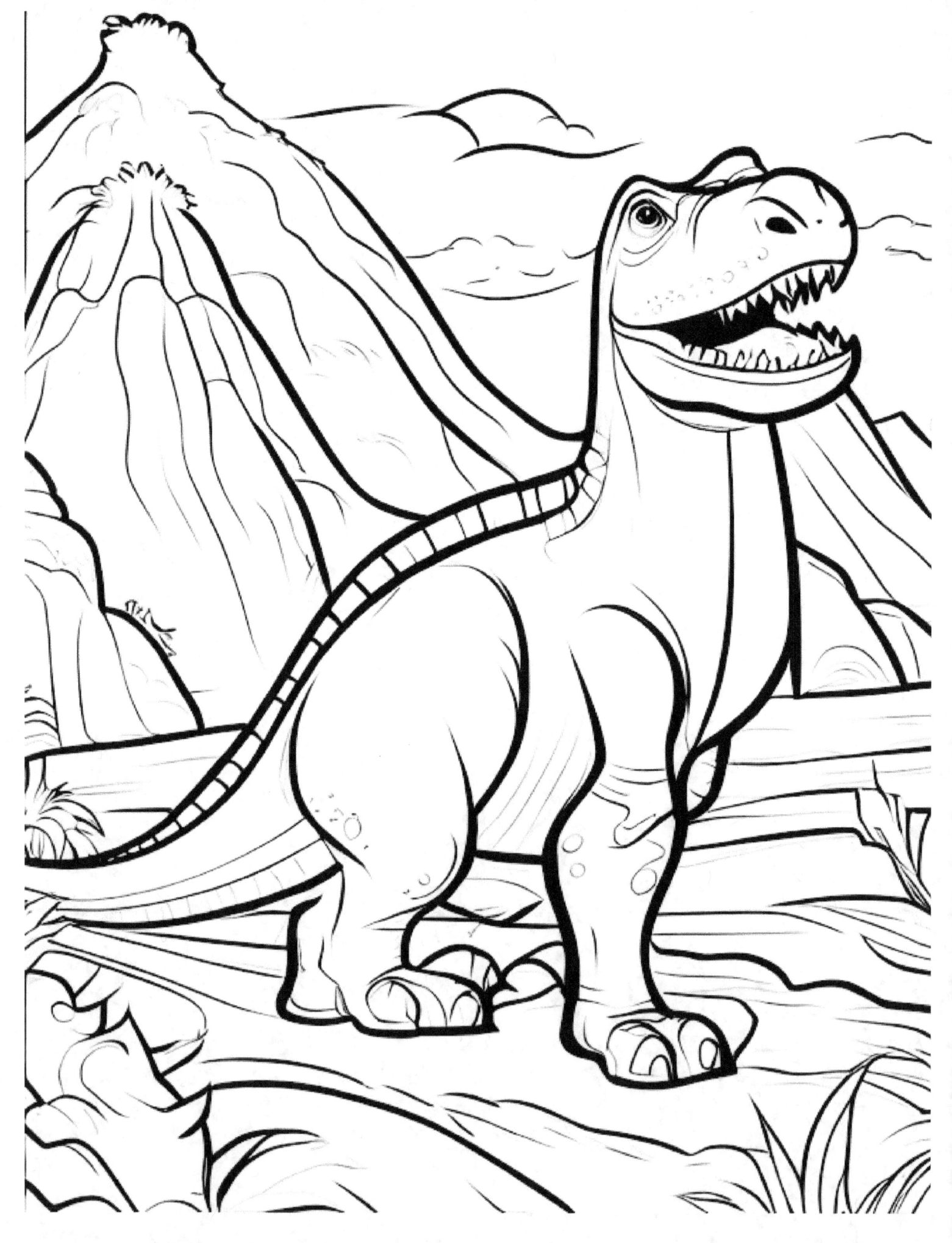

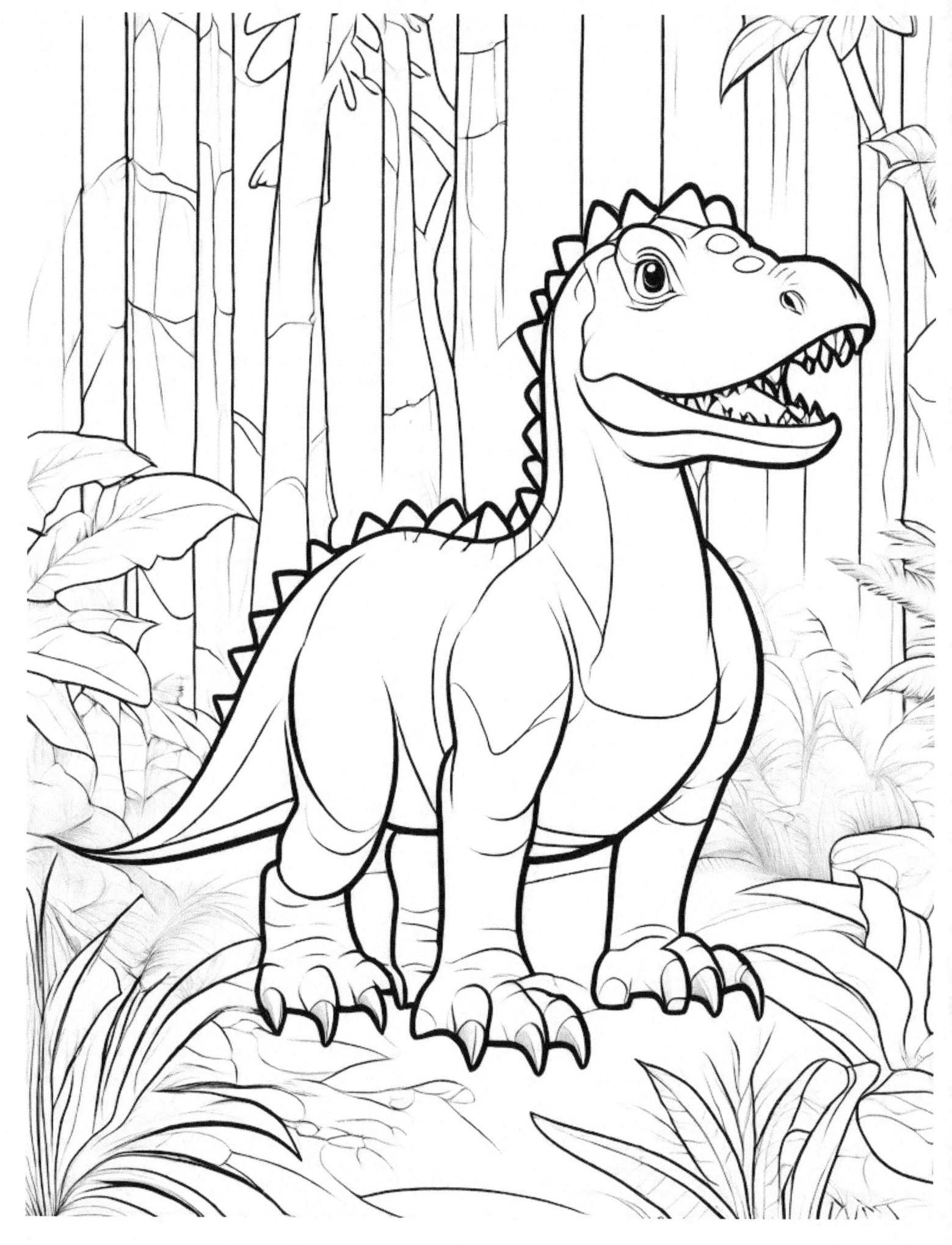

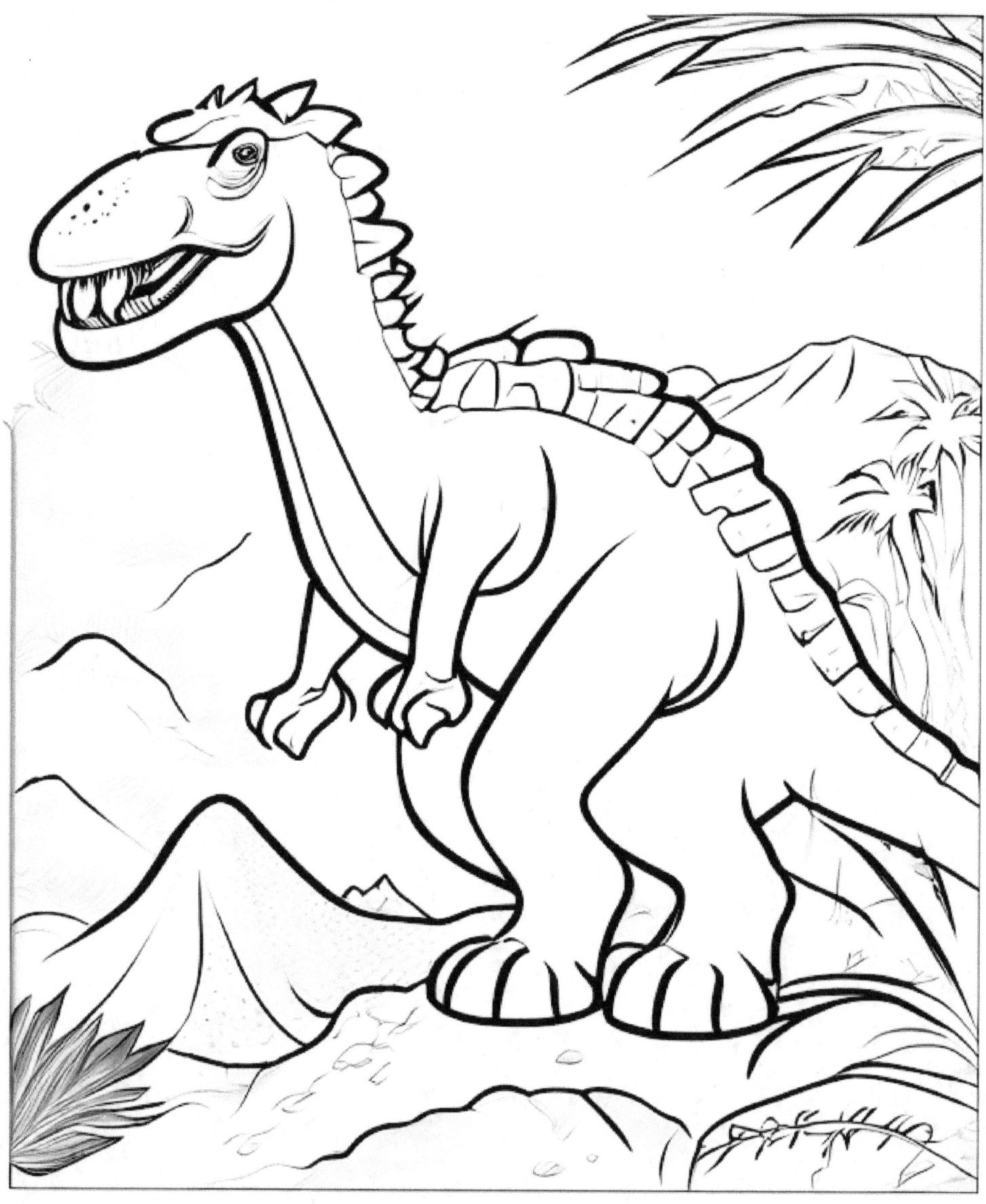

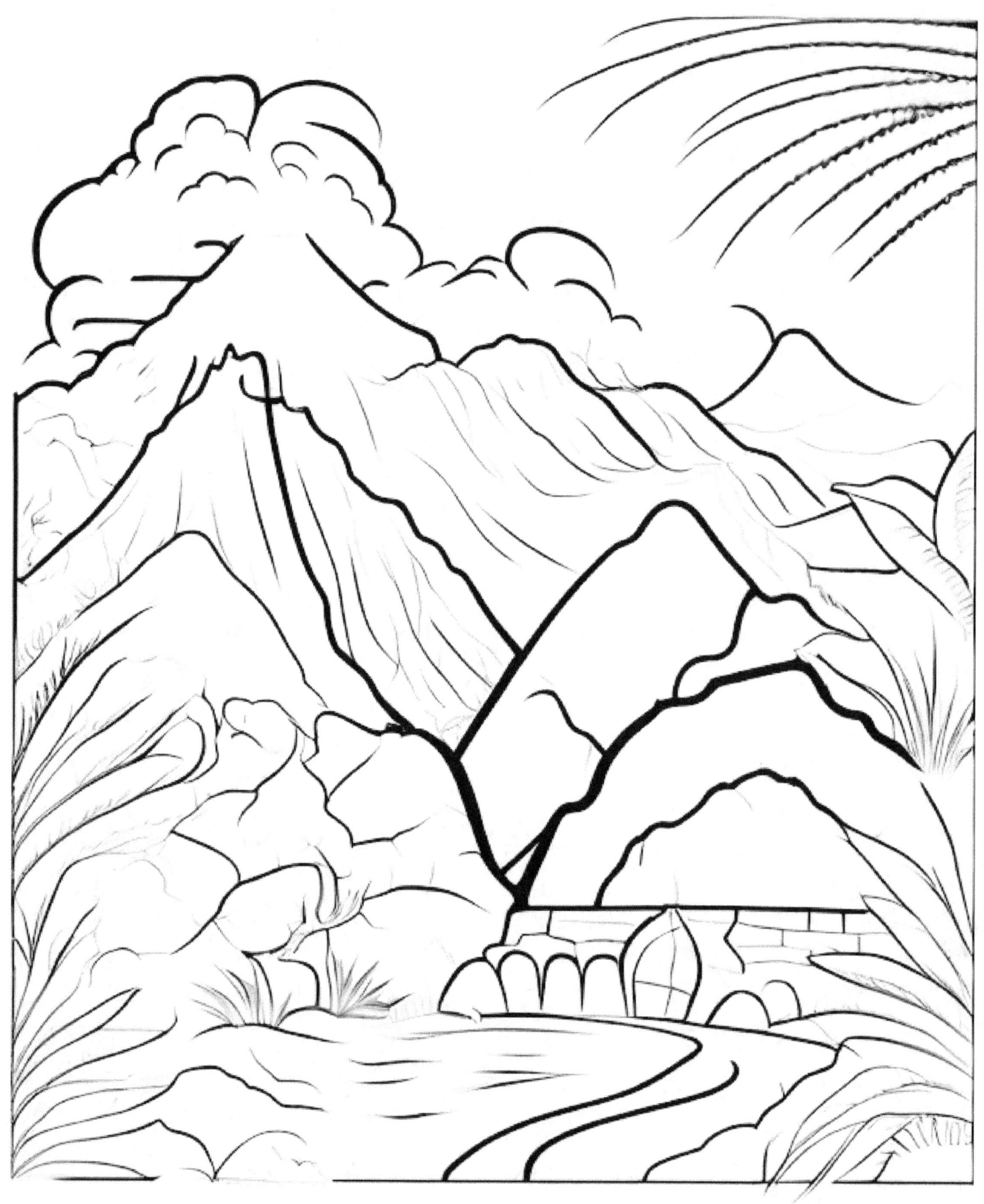

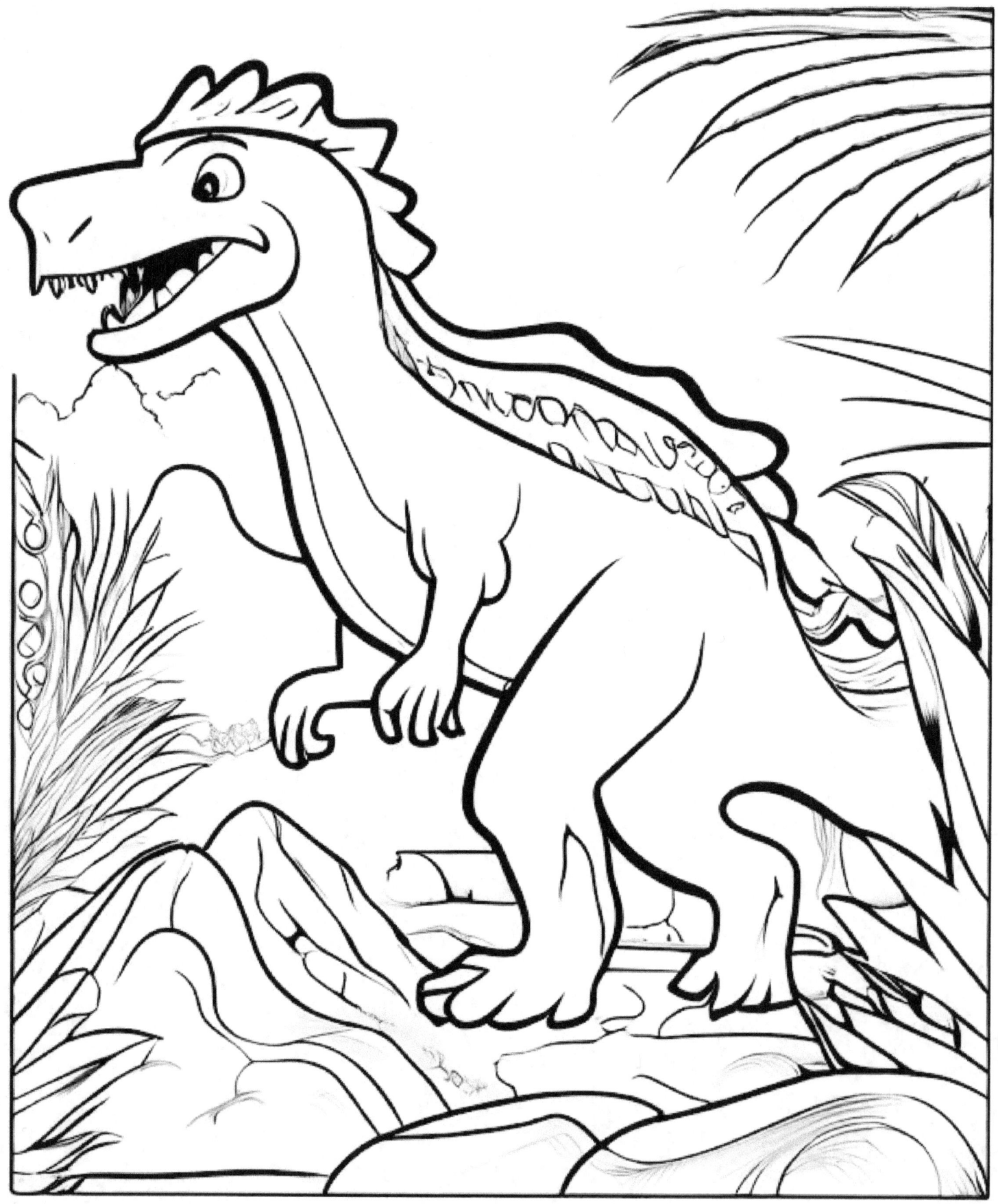

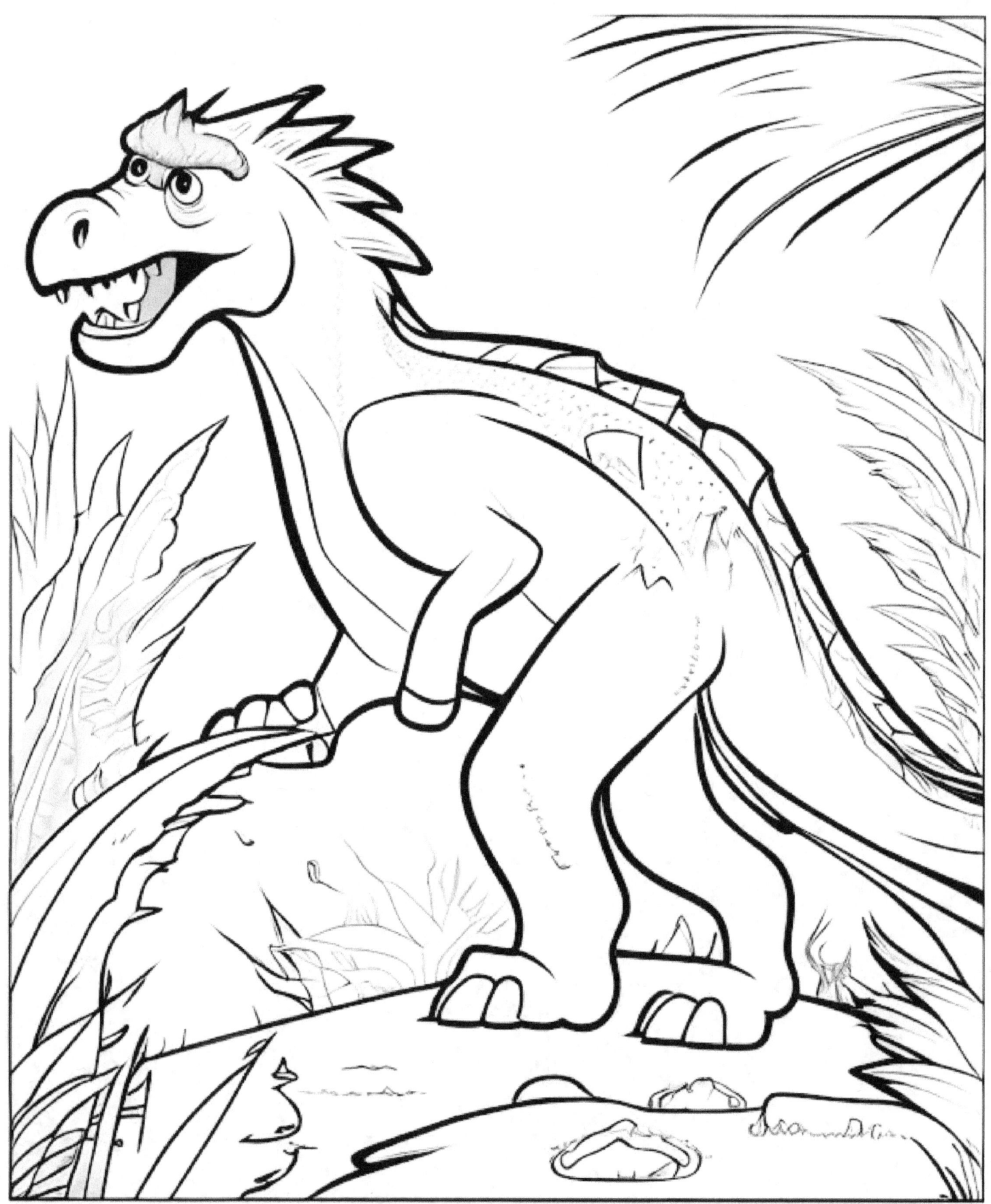

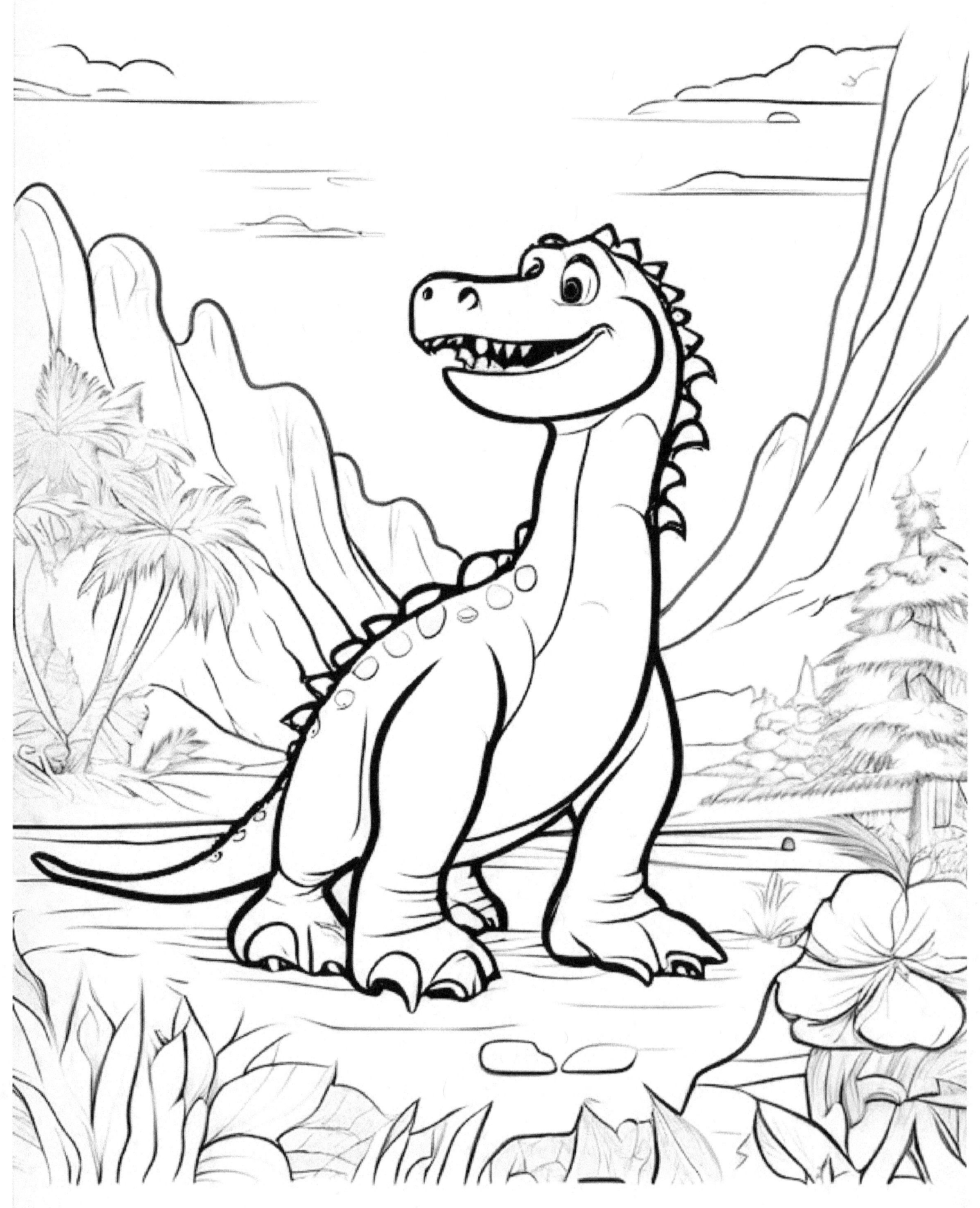

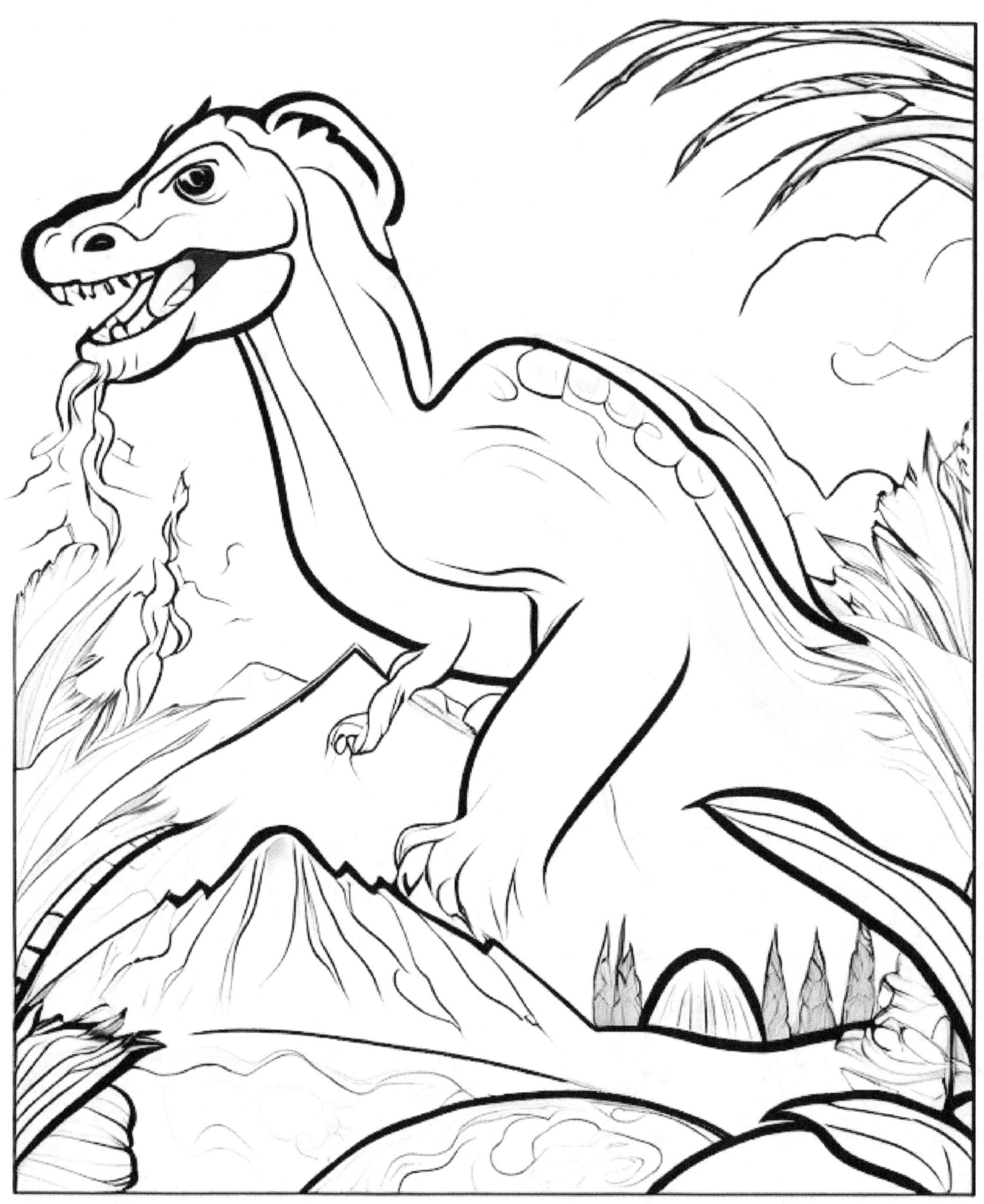

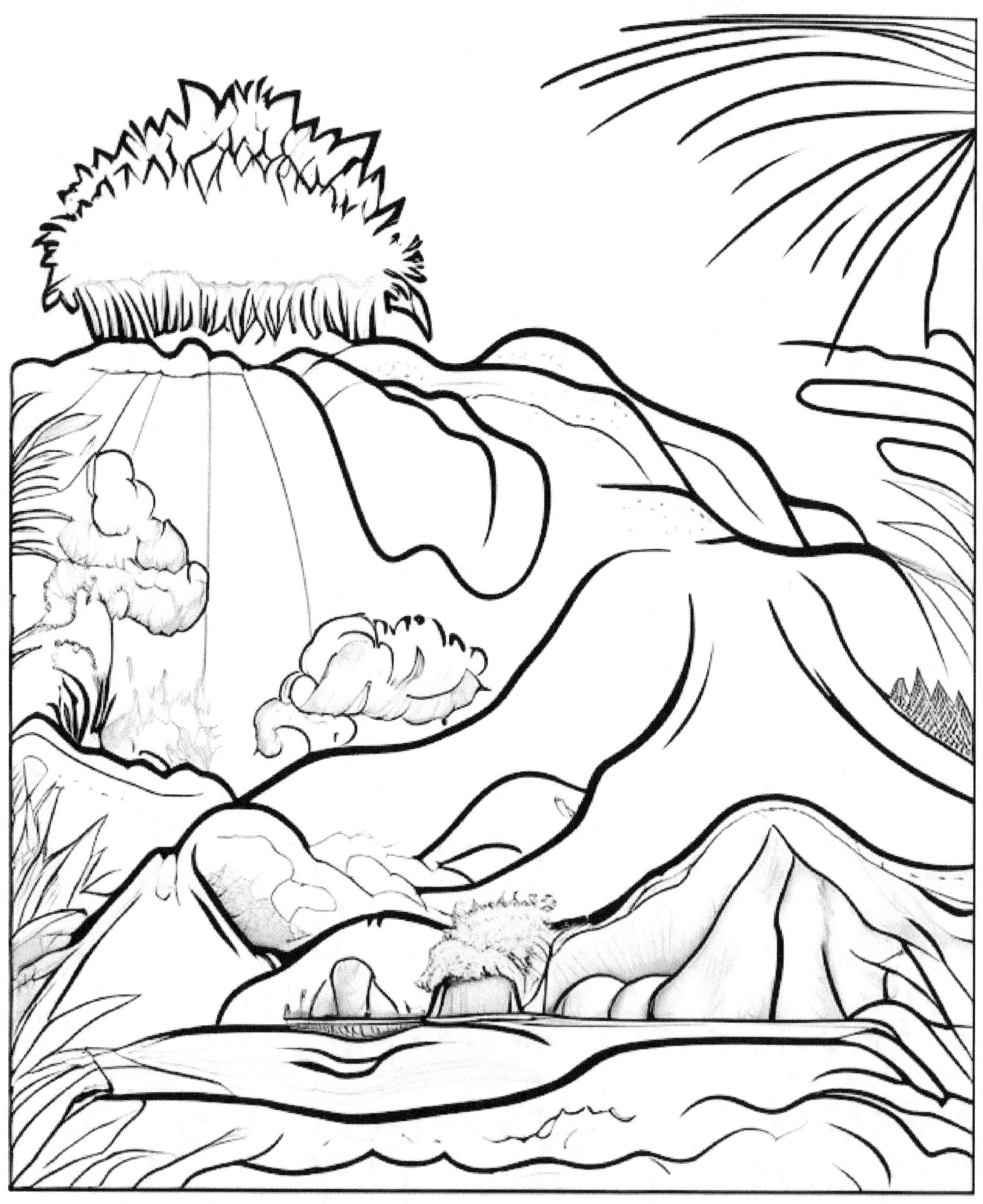

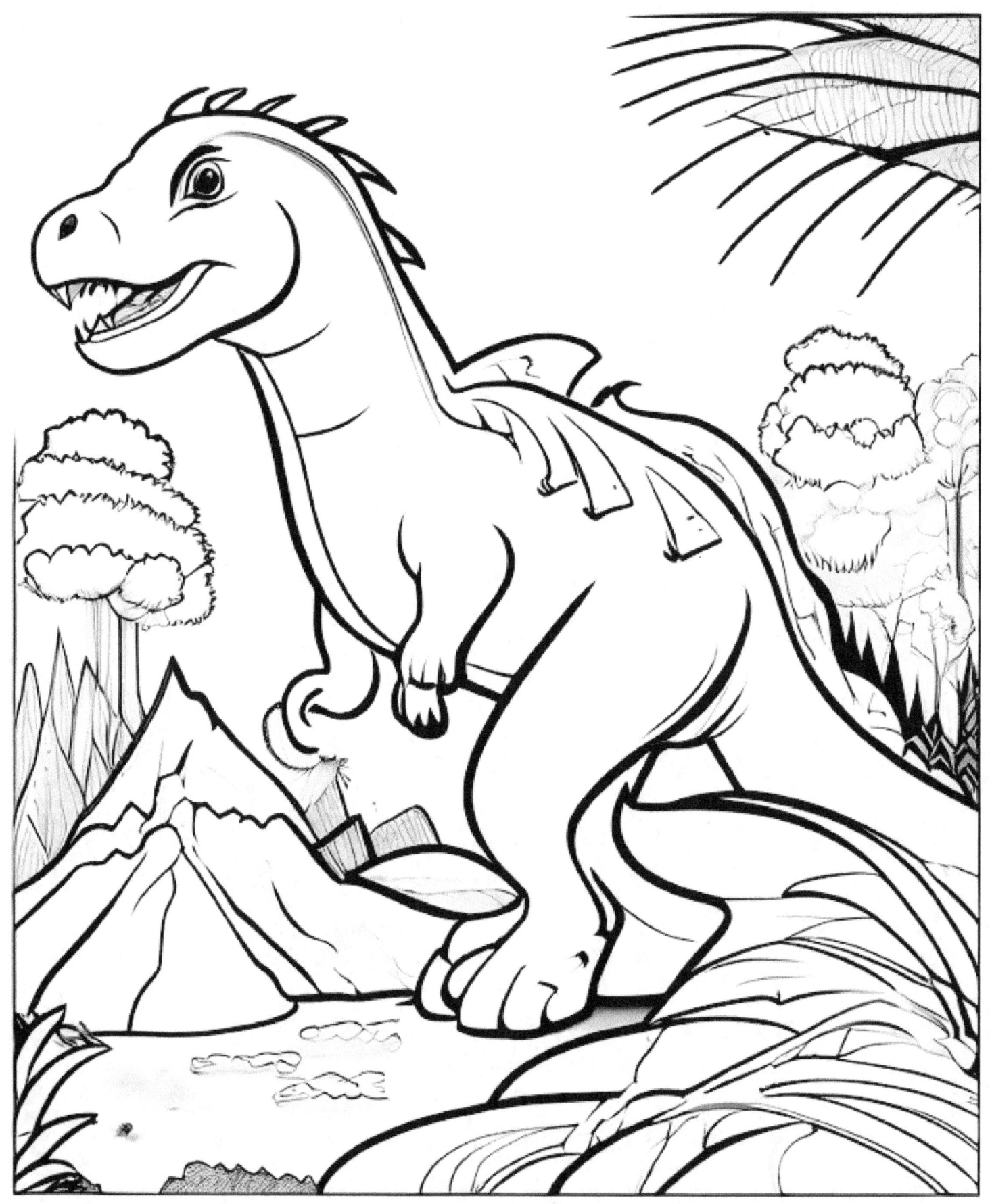

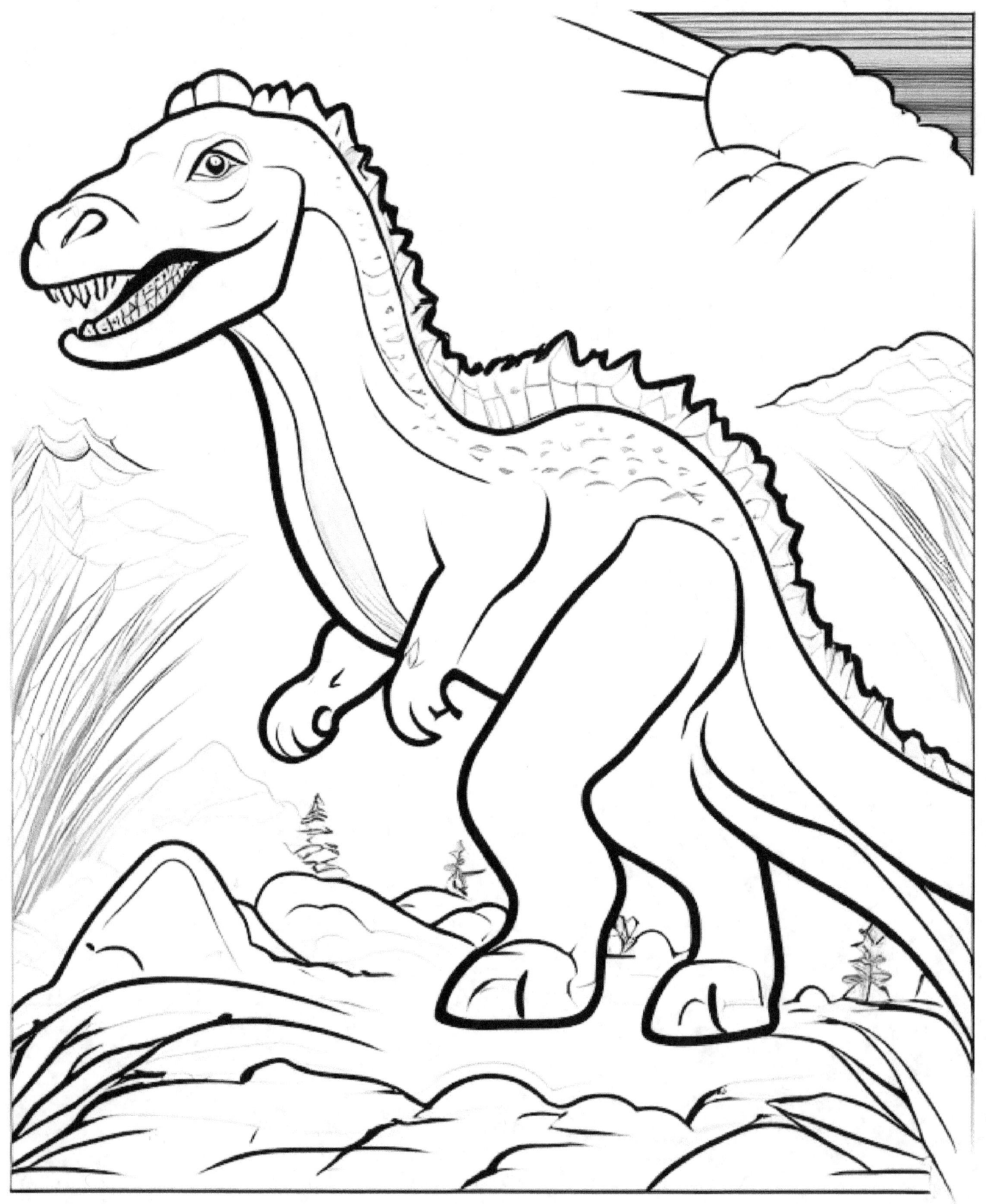

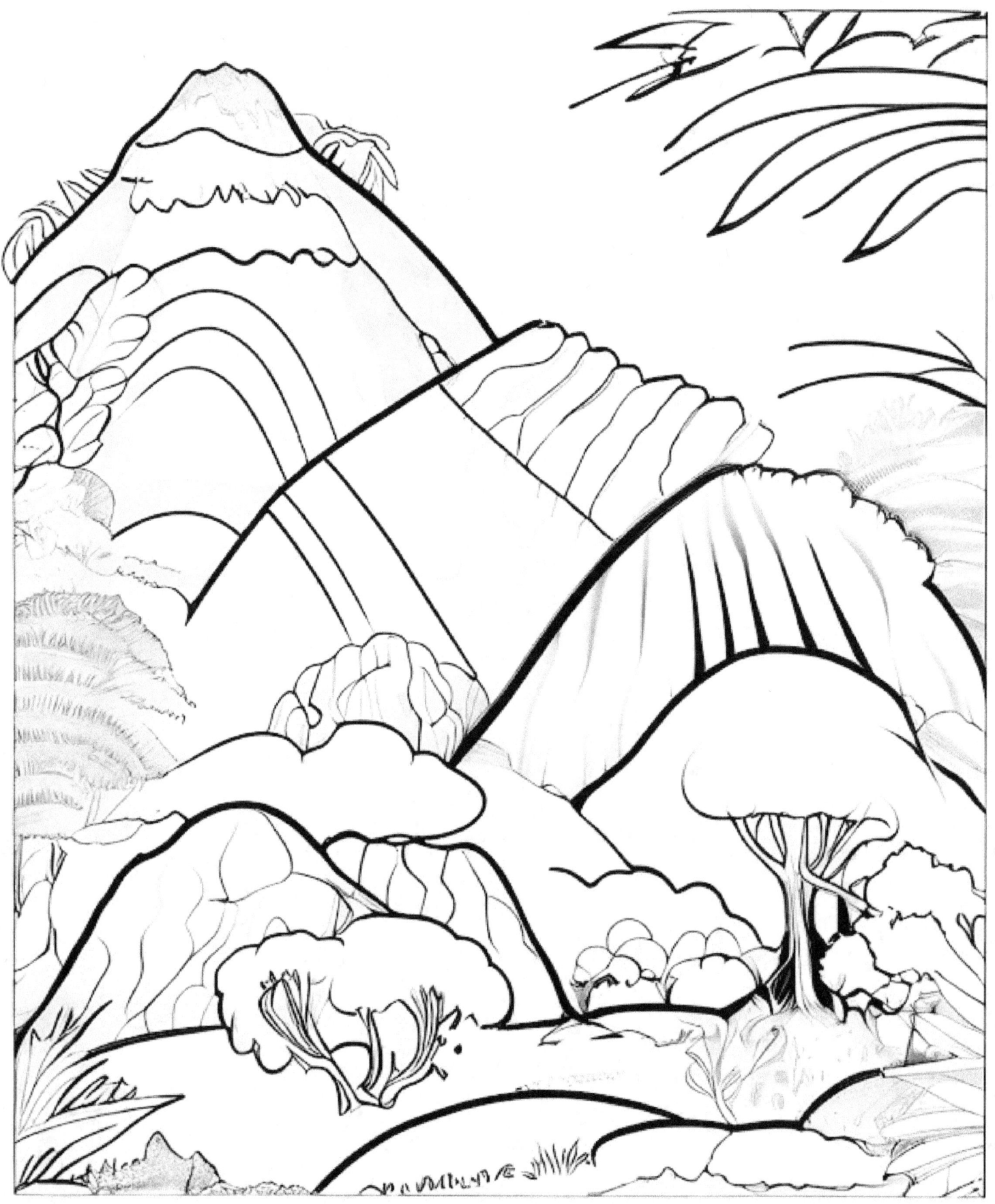

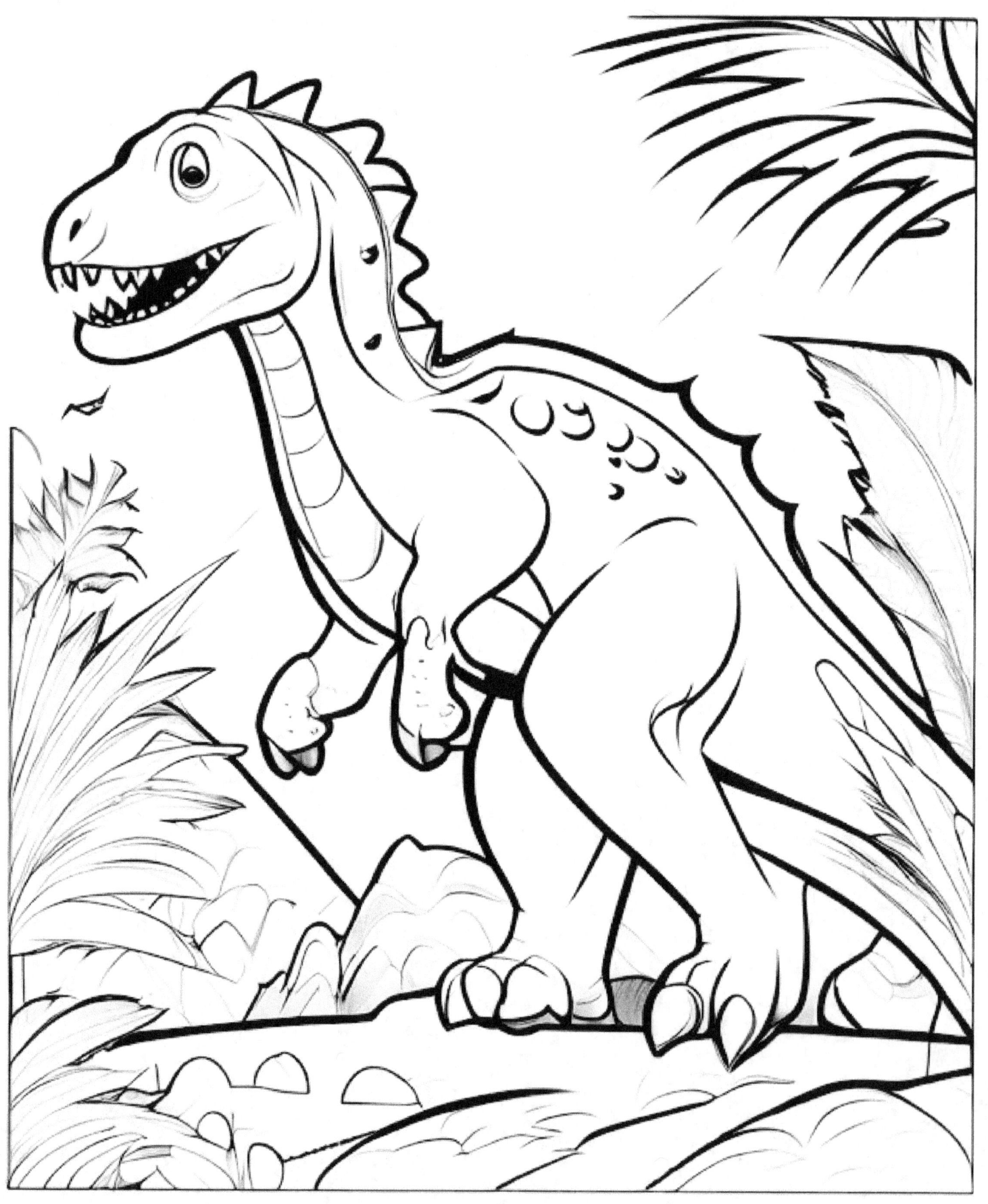

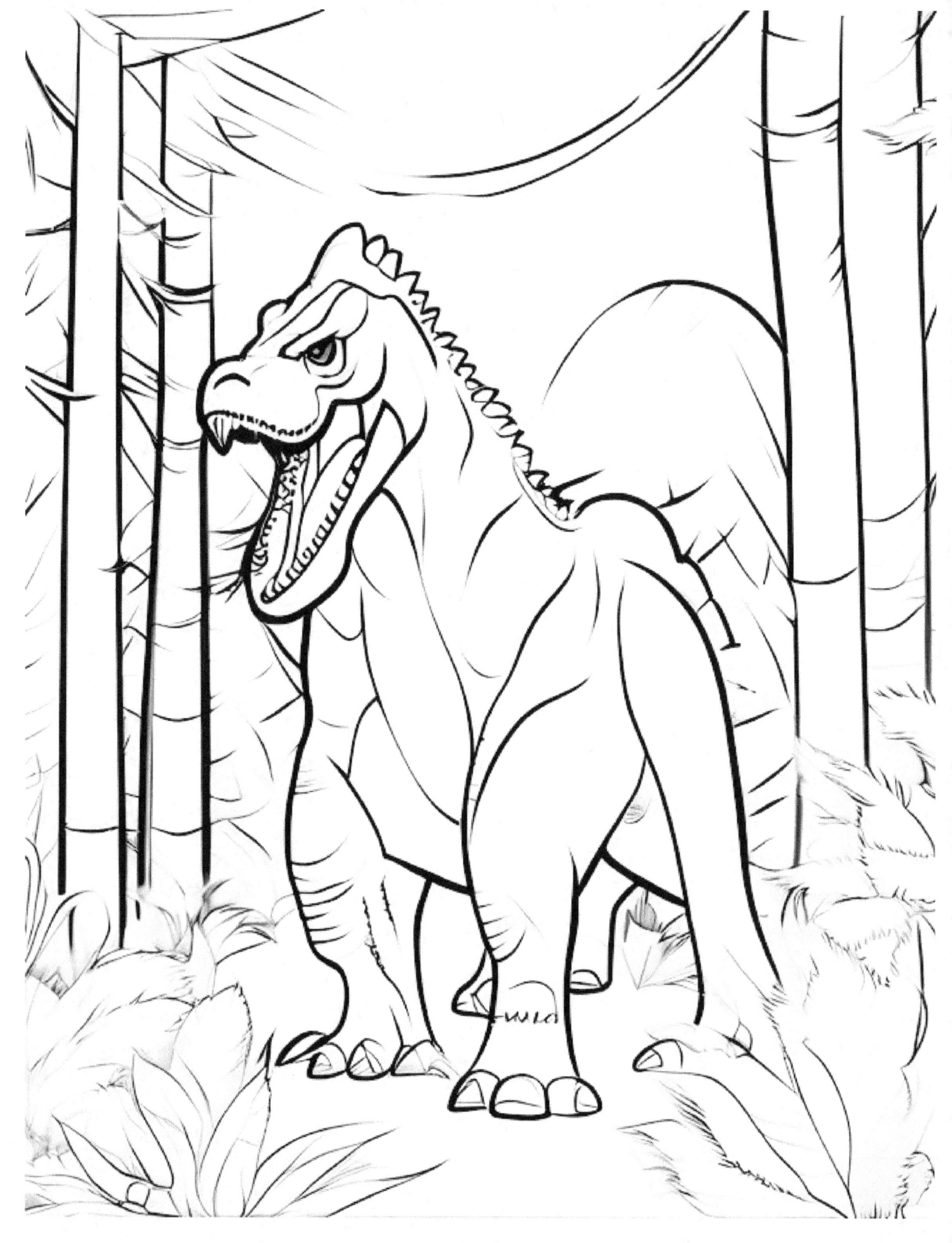

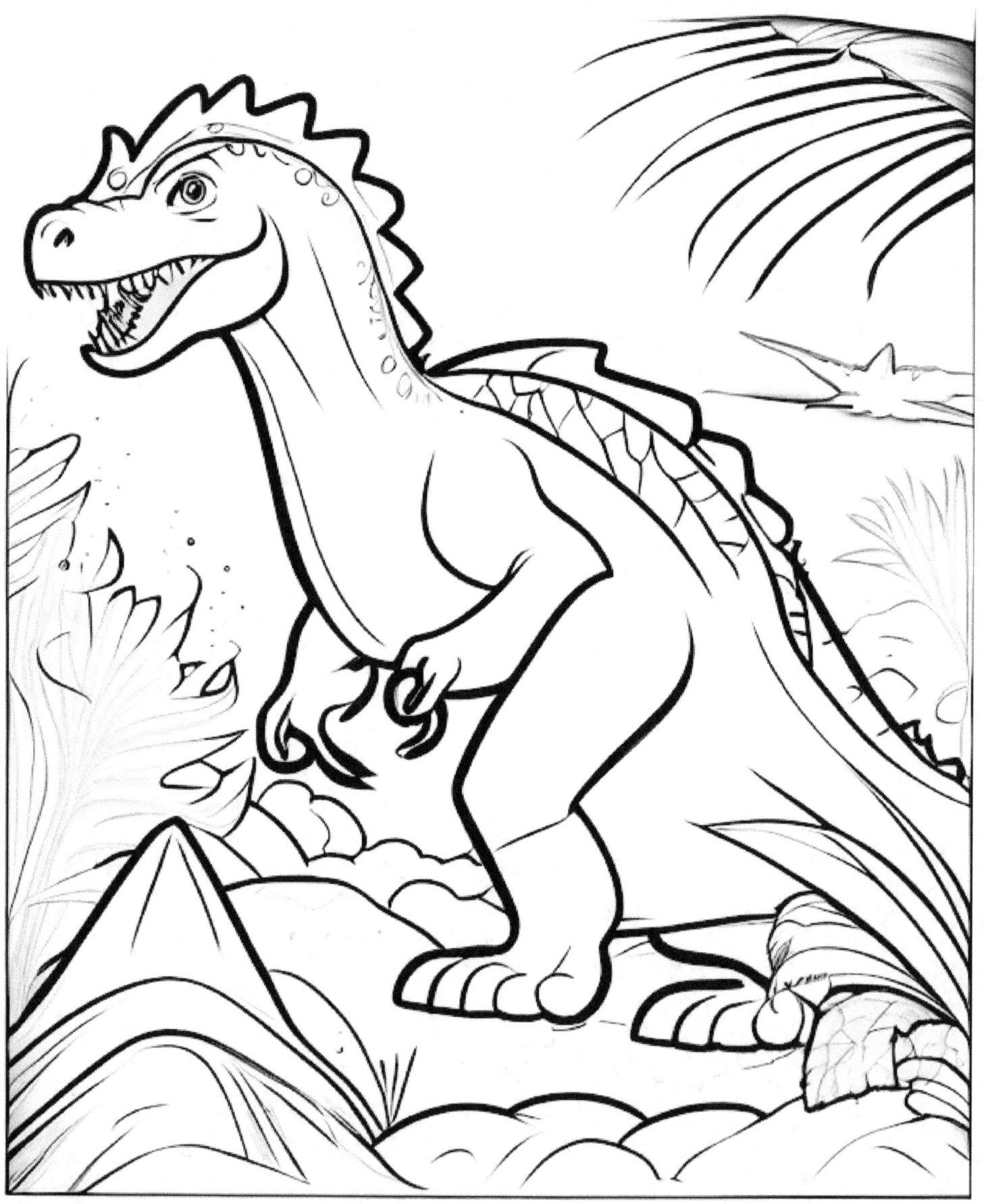

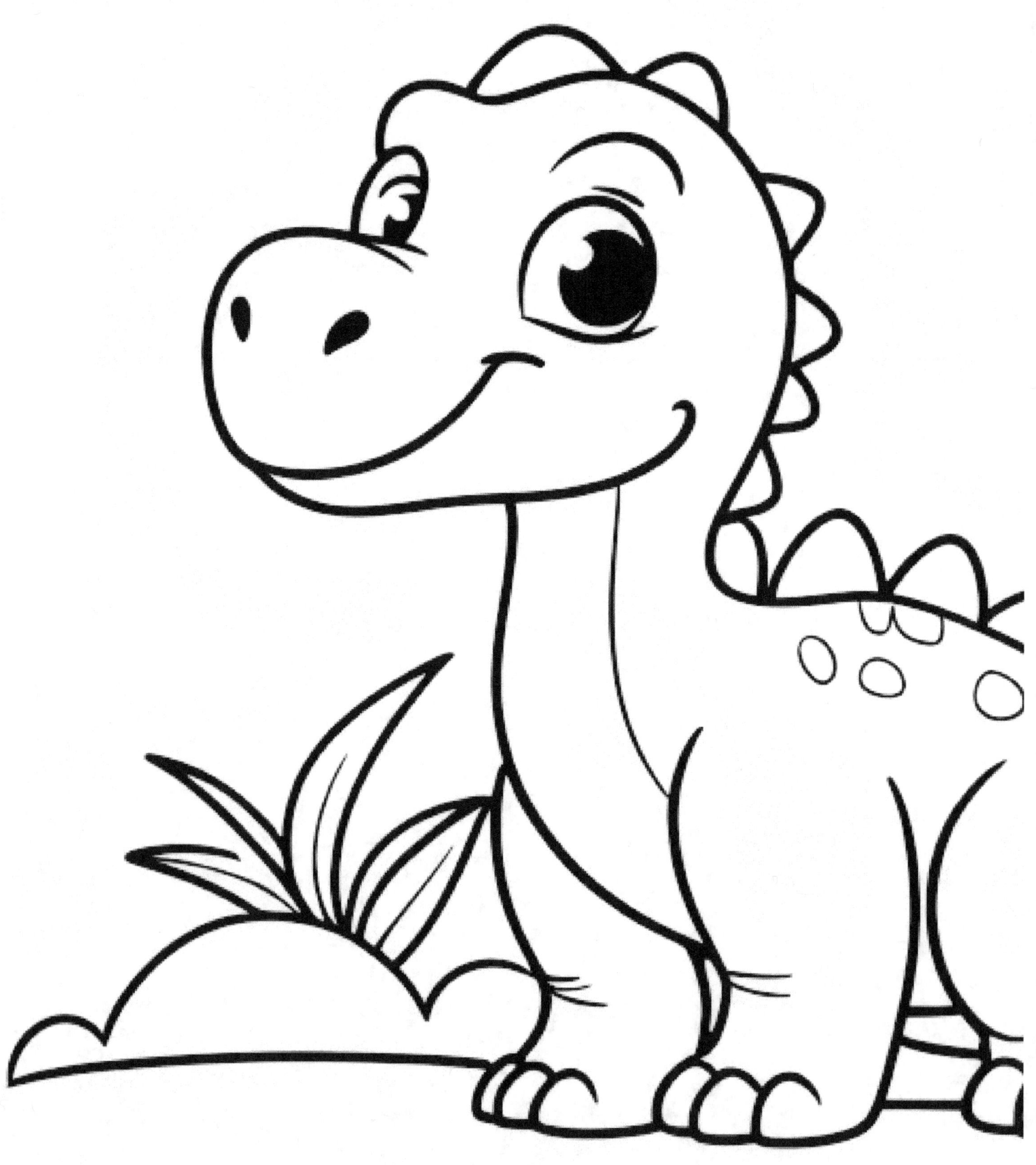

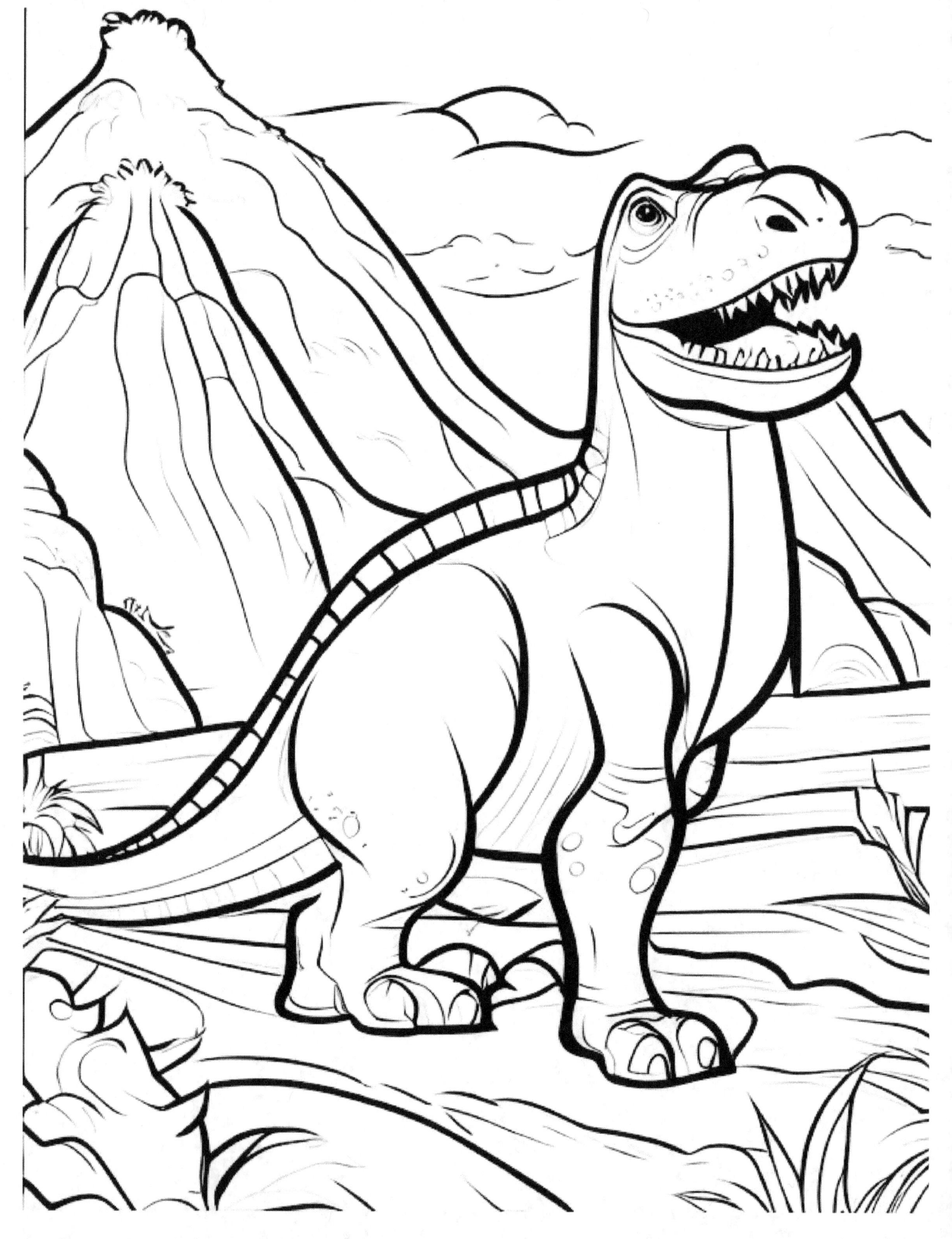

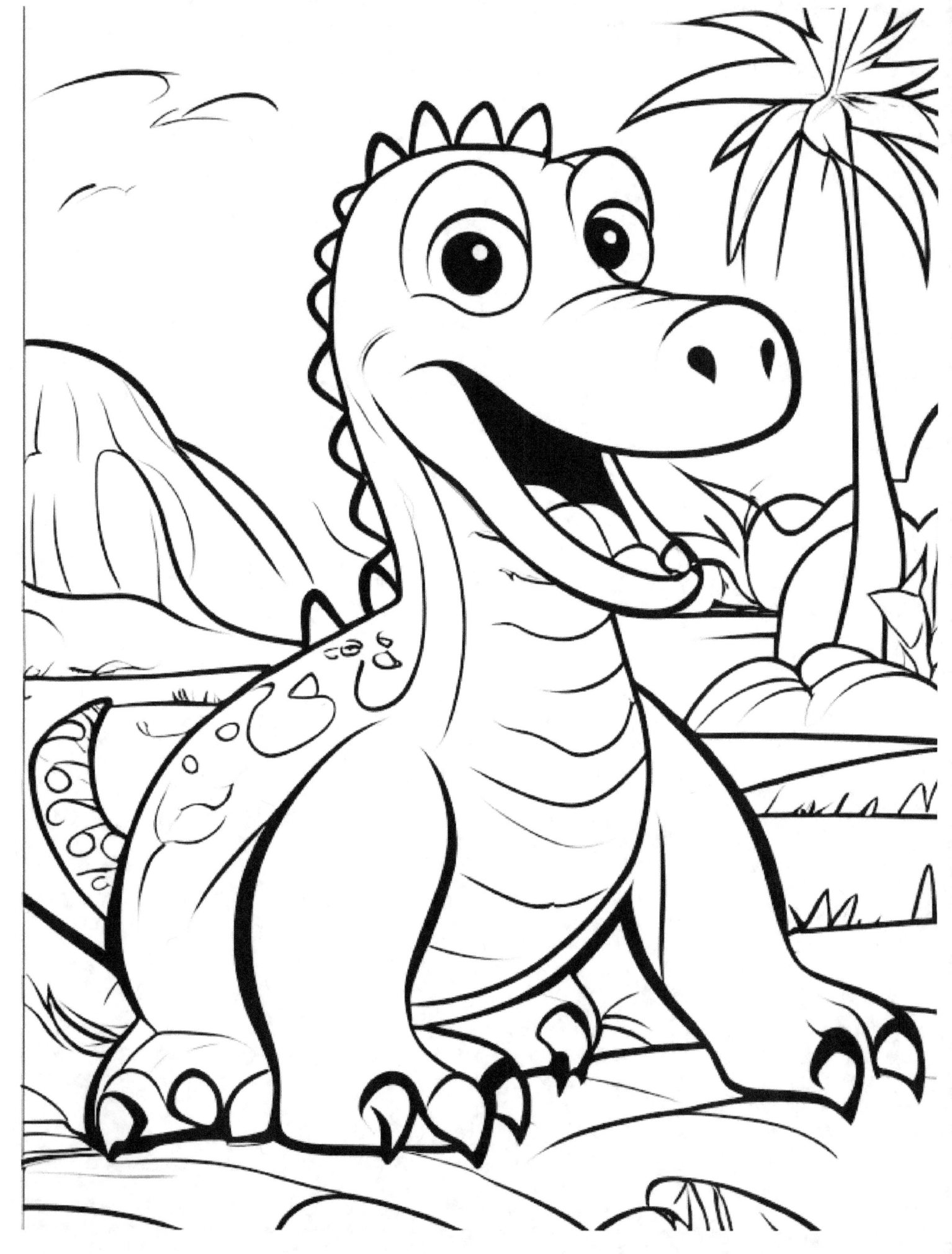

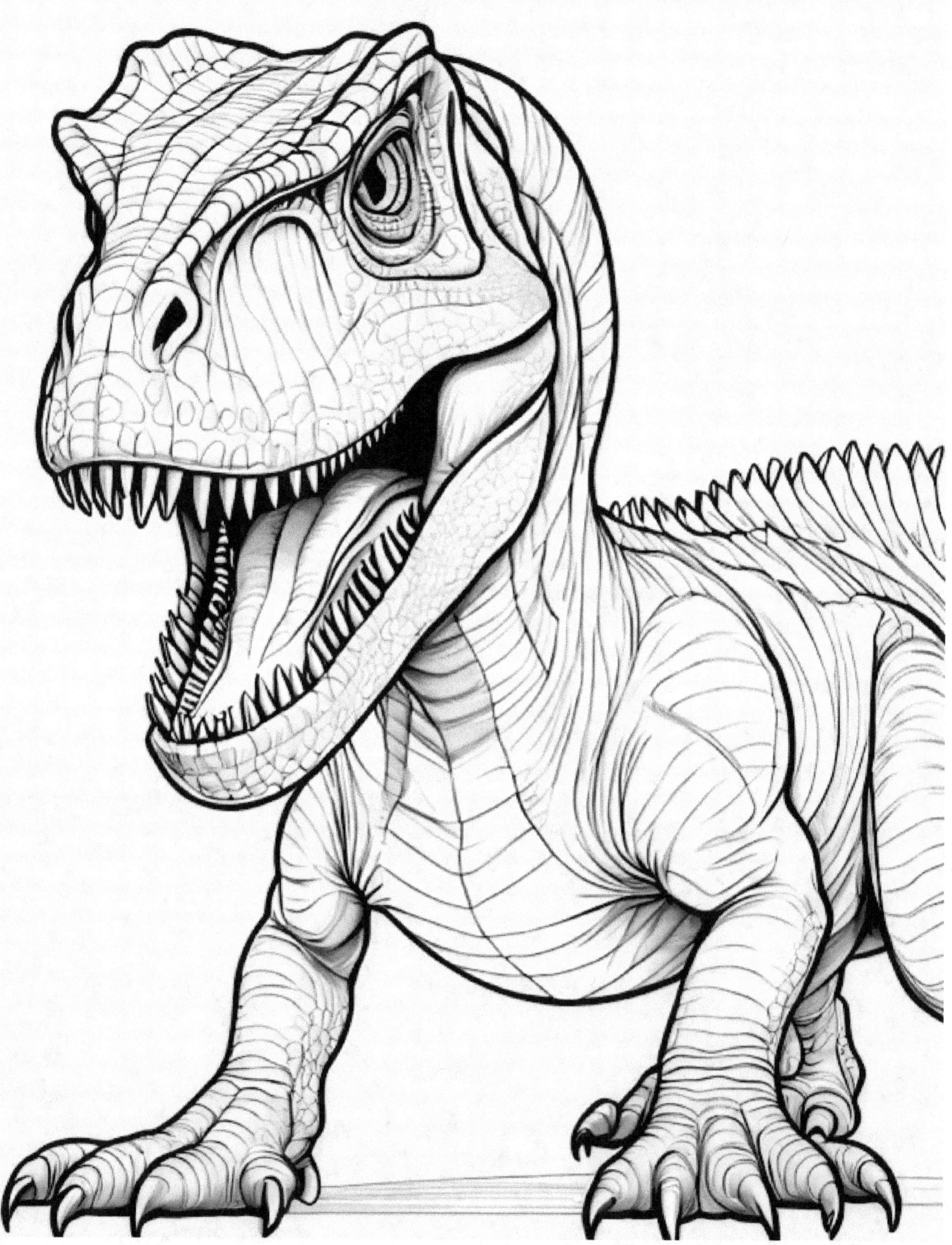

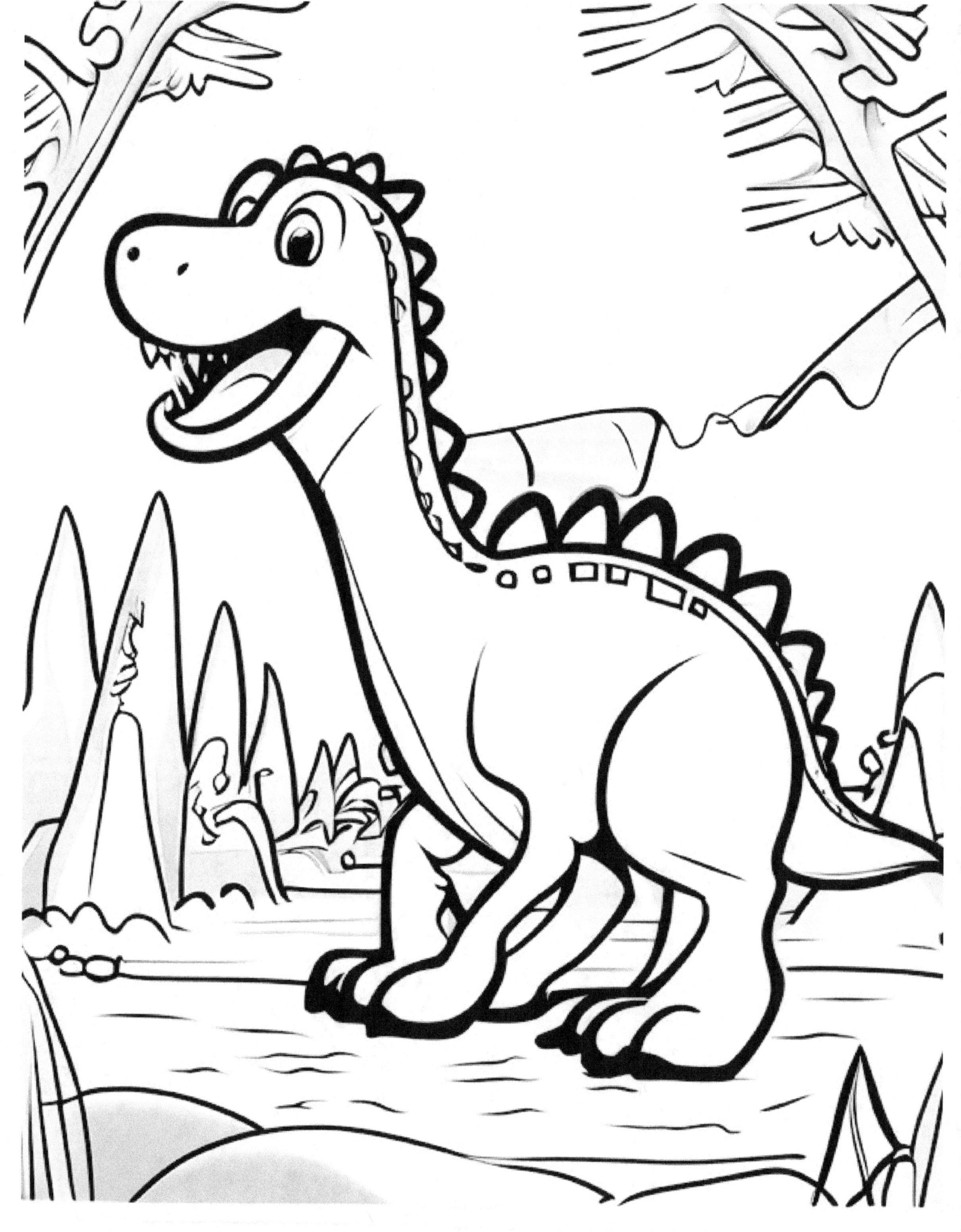

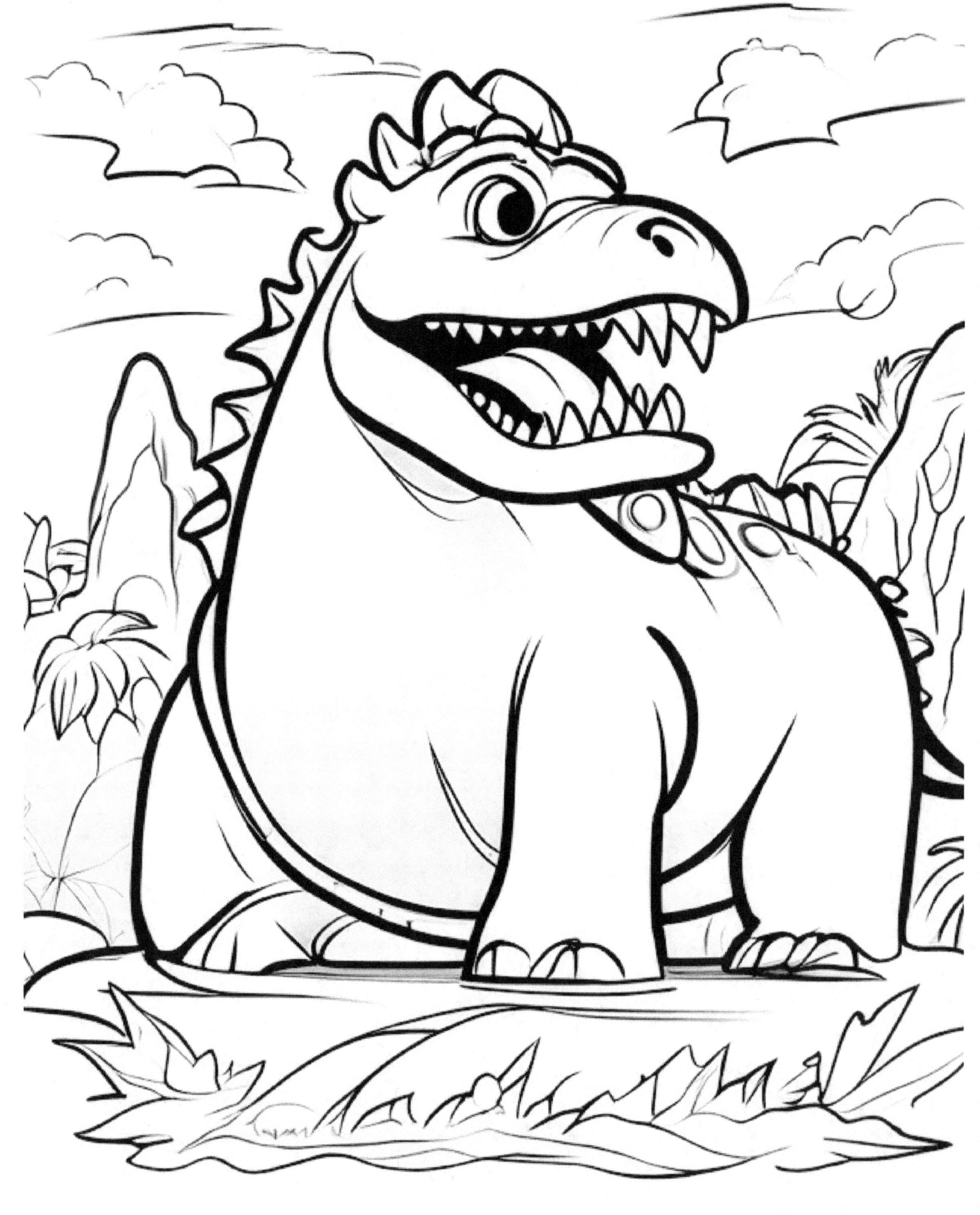

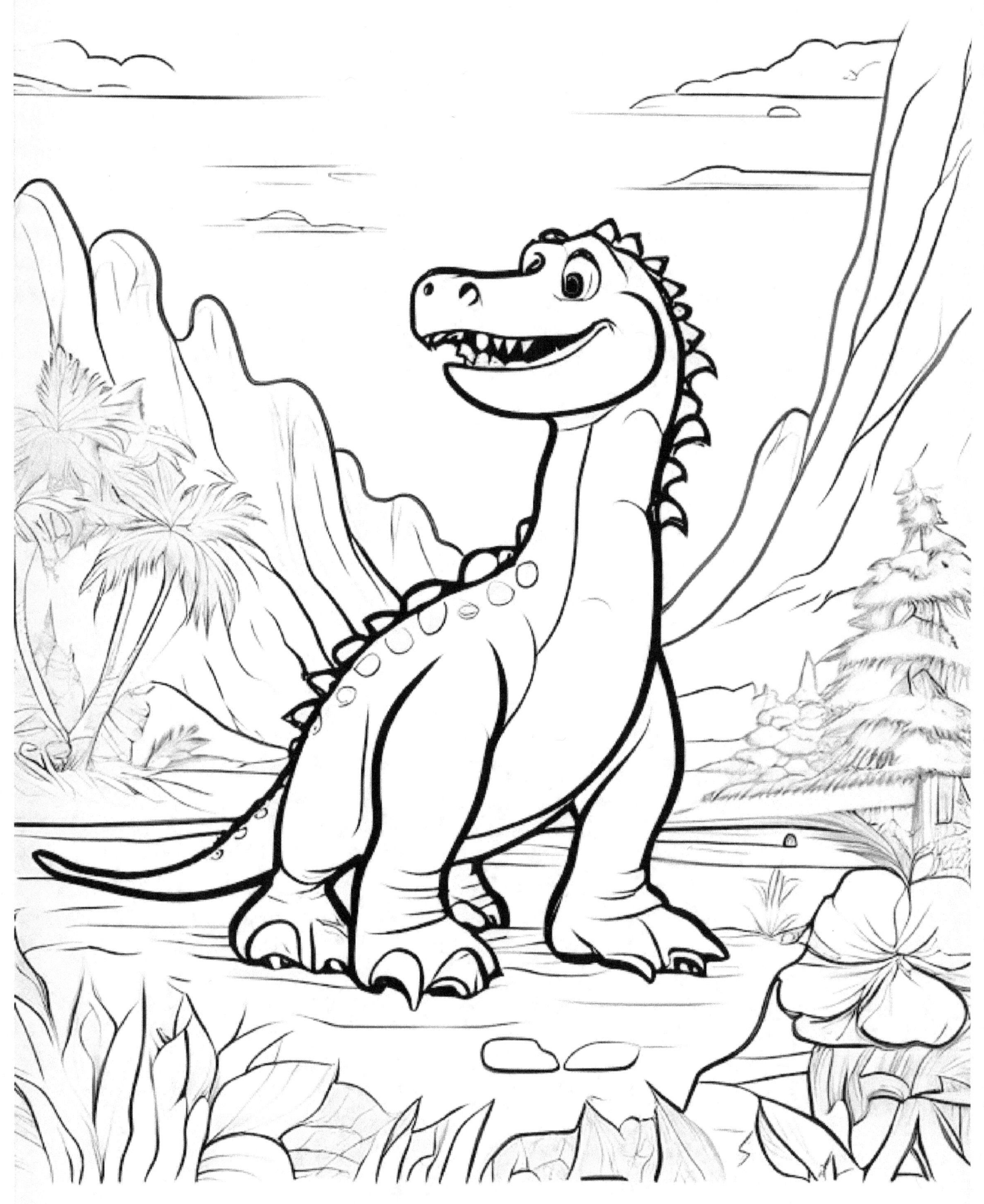

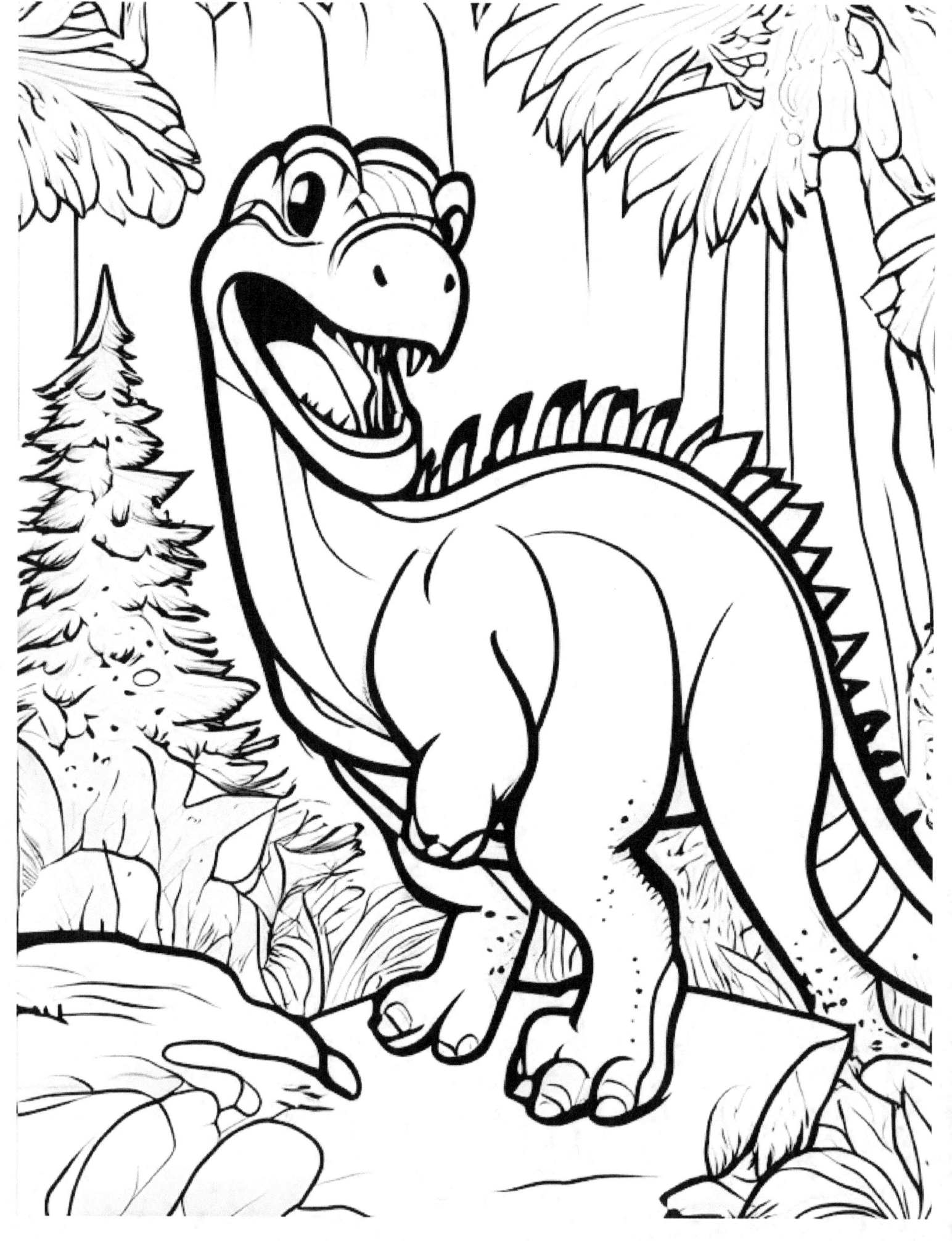

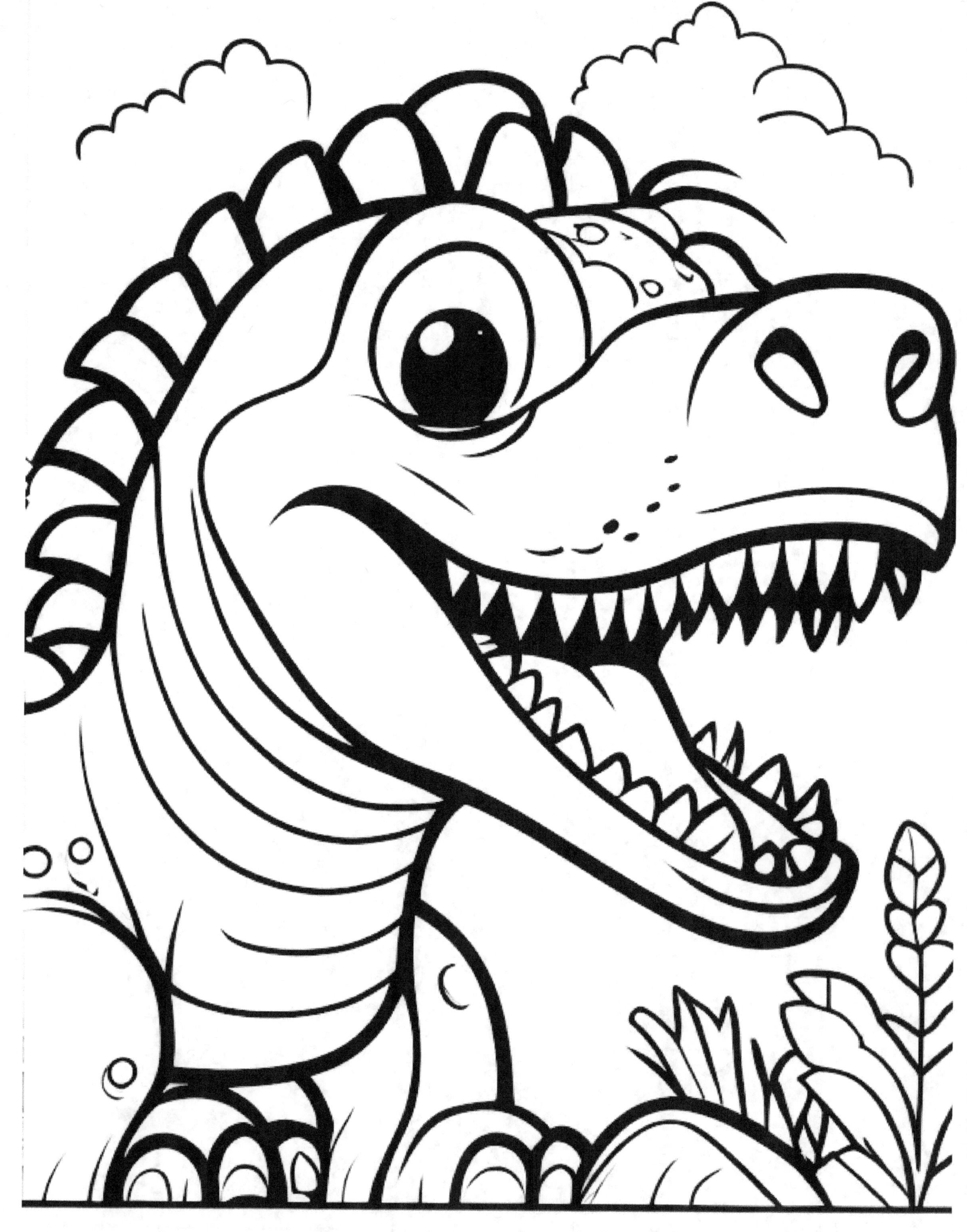

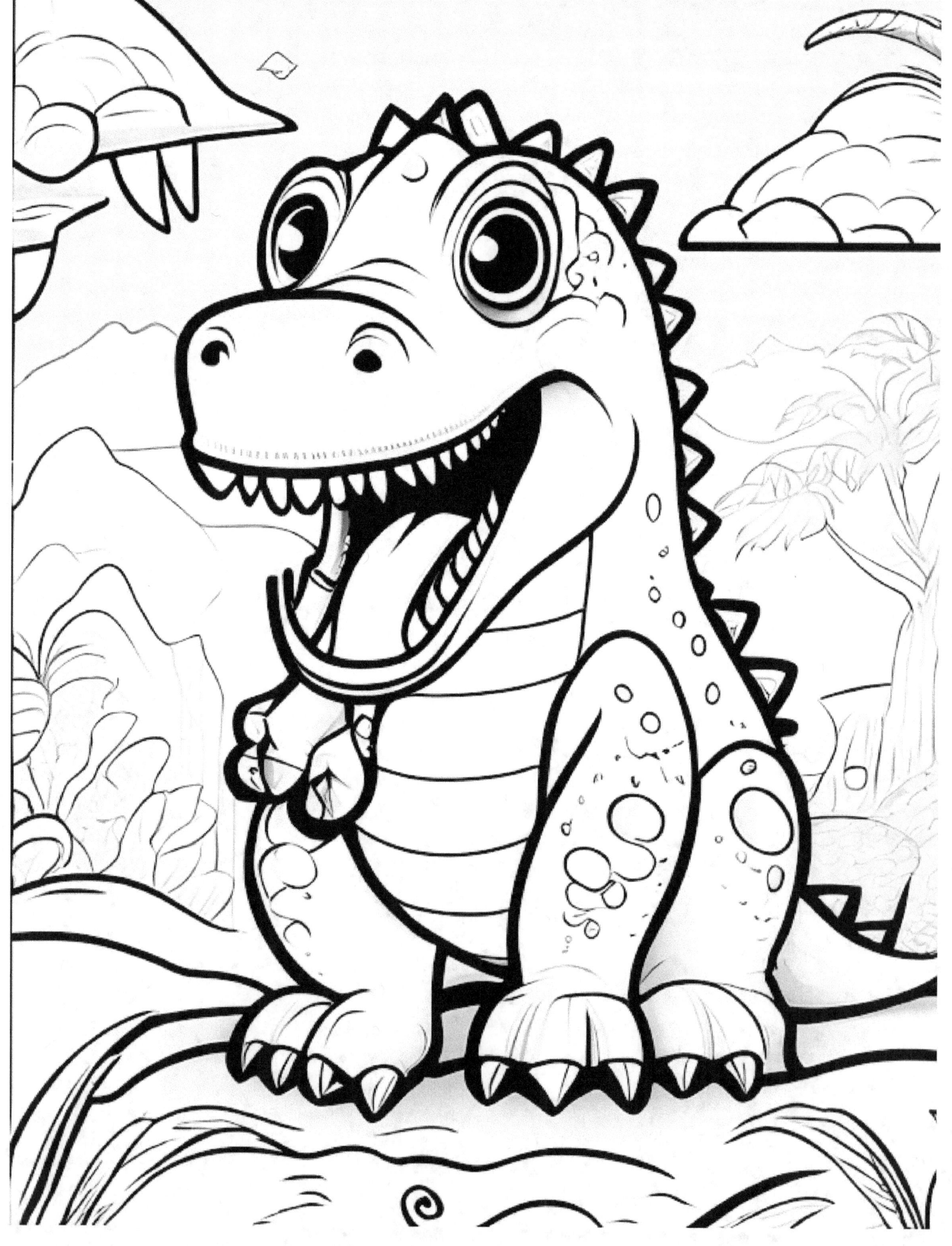

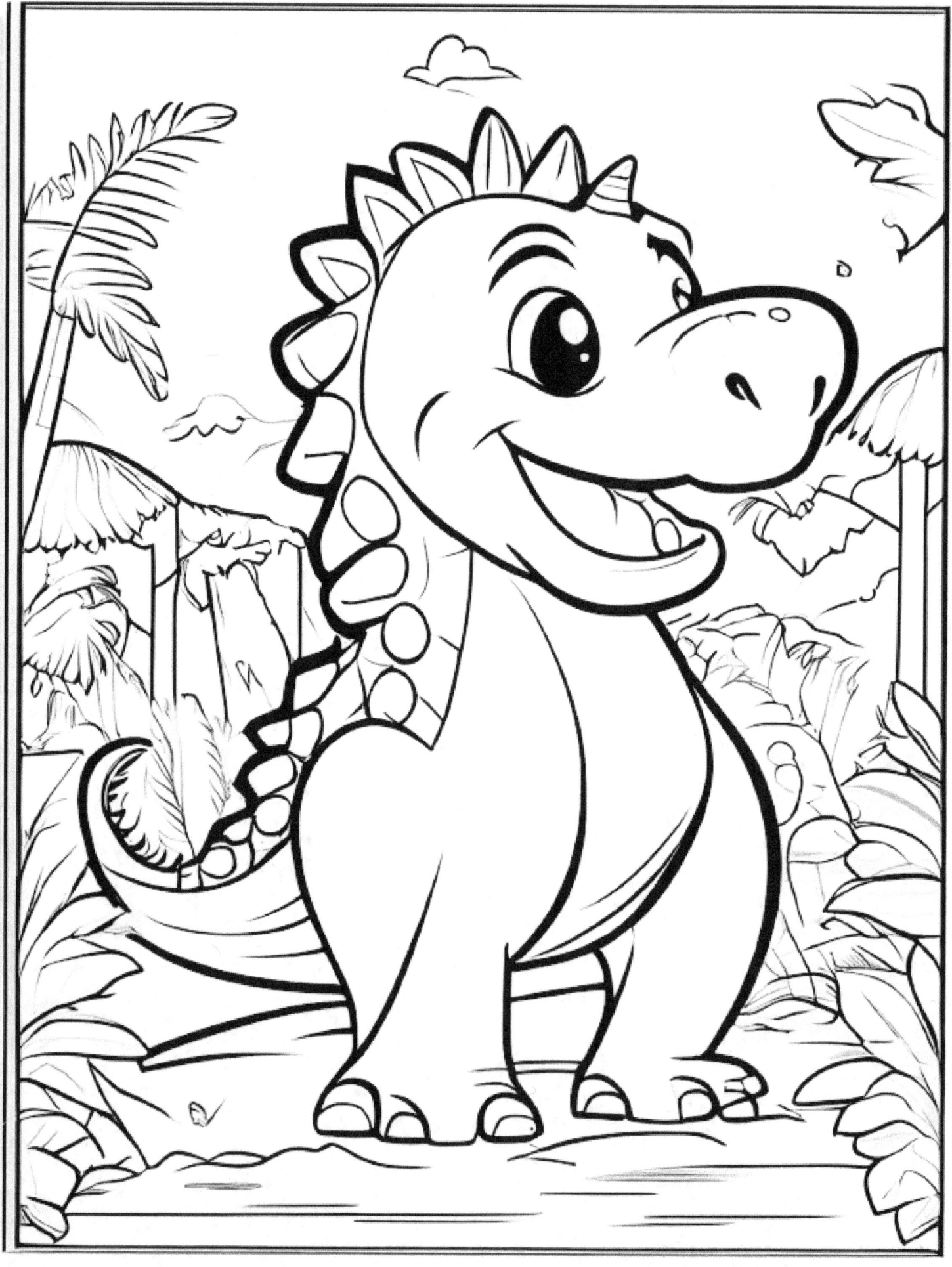

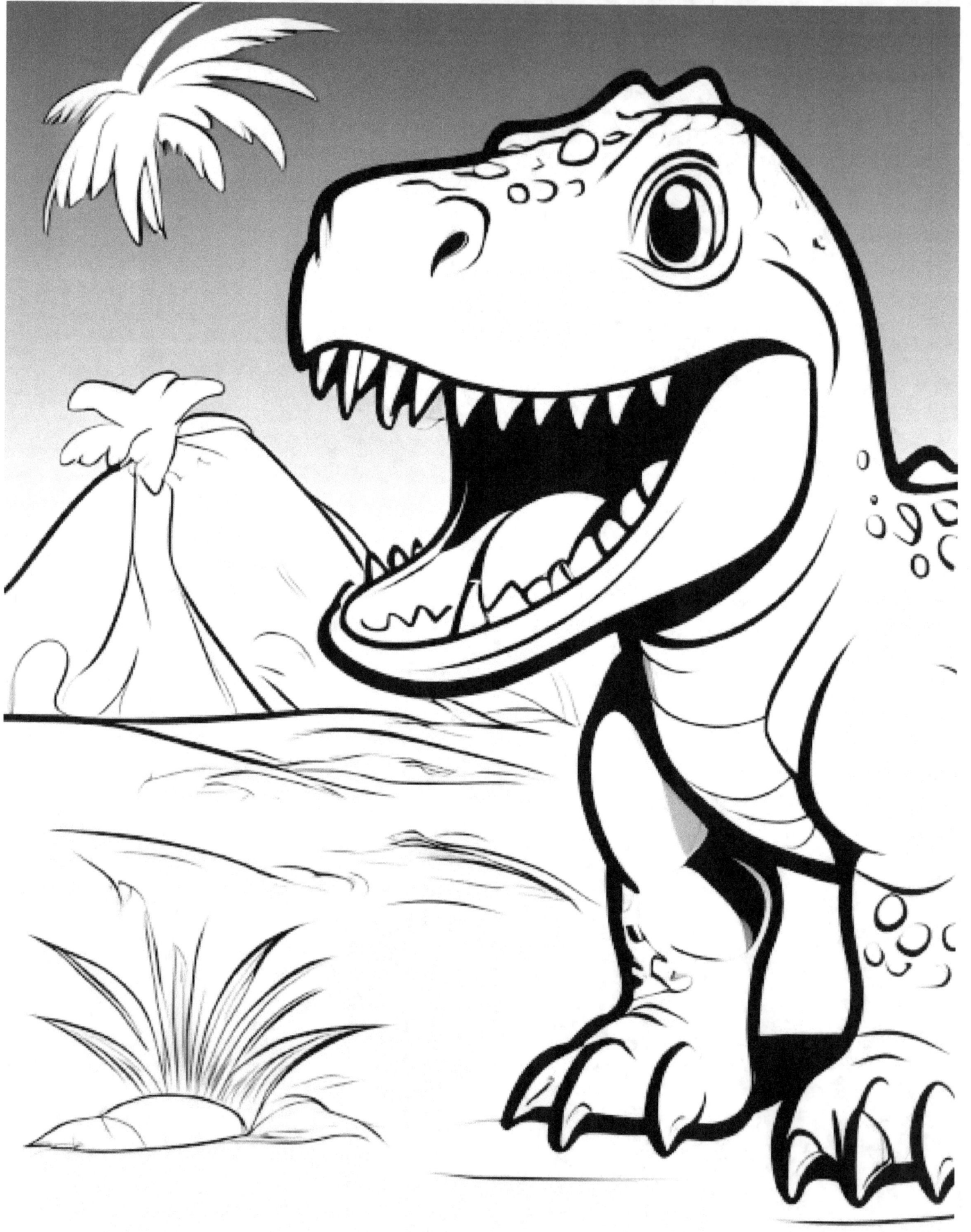

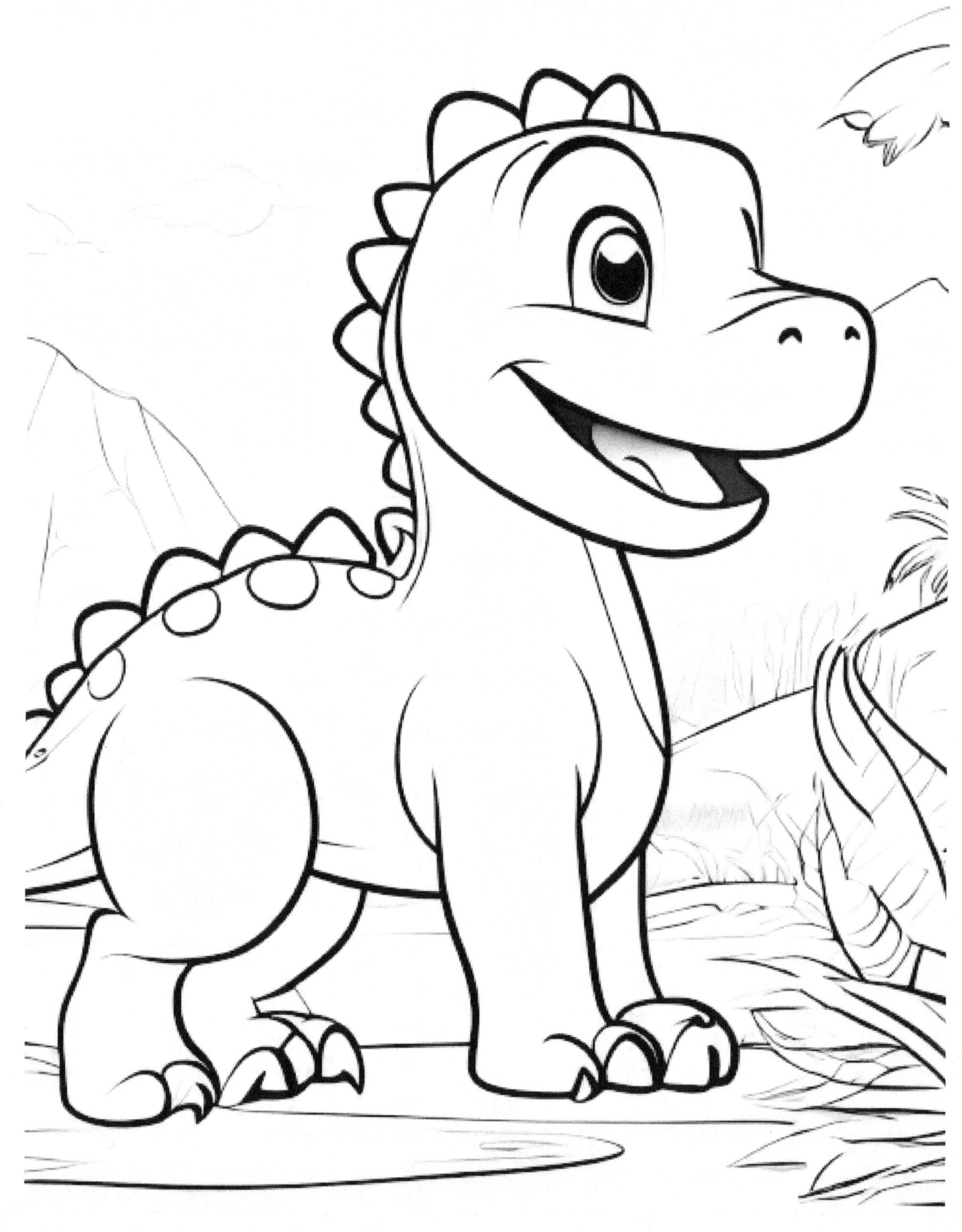

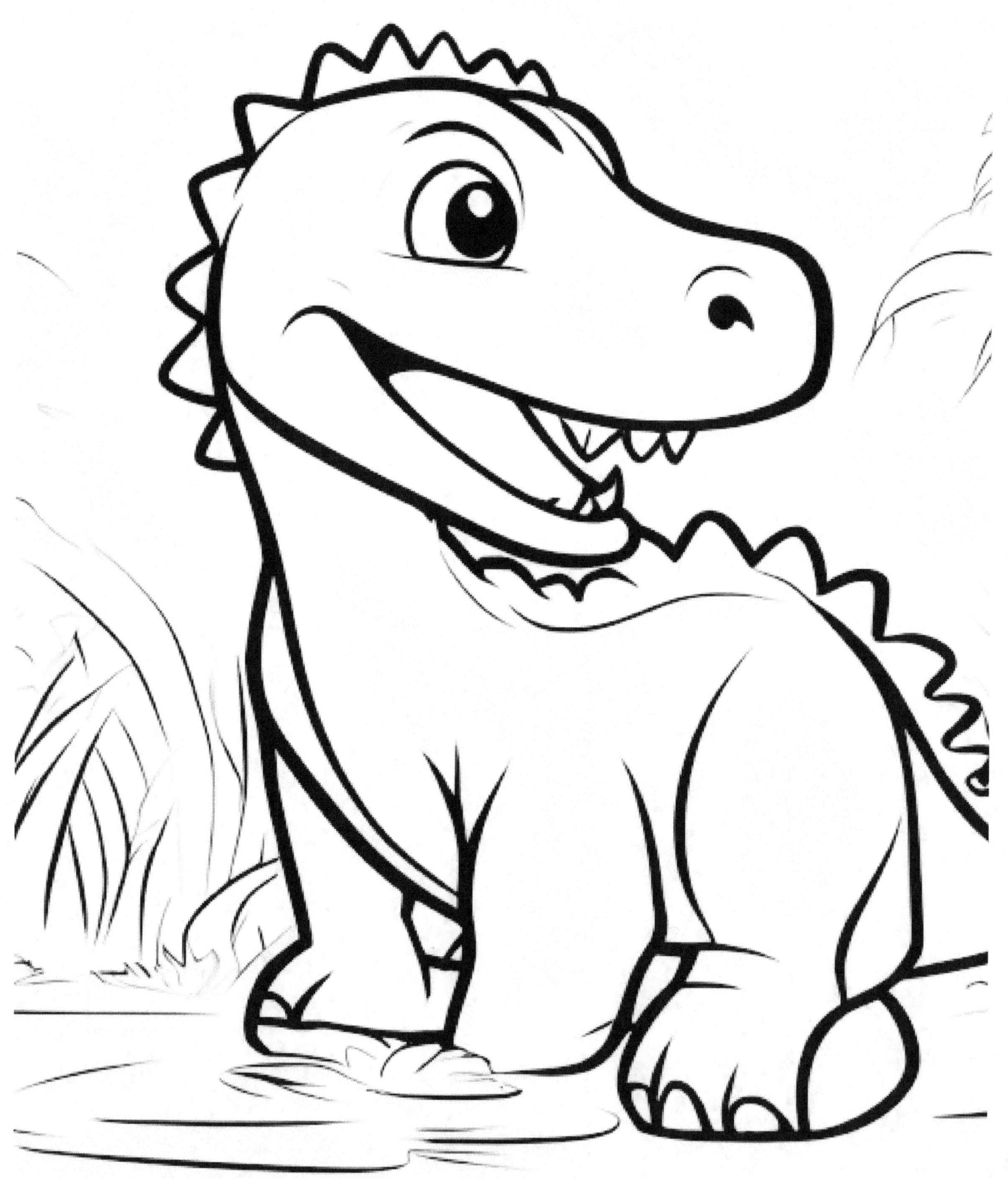